French Regional
Menus

Great Meals in Minutes was created by Rebus Inc., and
published by Time-Life Books.

This edition published 1995 by Bloomsbury Books, an
imprint of The Godfrey Cave Group, 42 Bloomsbury Street,
London, WC1B 3QJ.

© 1995 Time-Life Books BV.

ISBN 1 85471 566 6

Printed and bound in Great Britain.

French Regional Menus

Bloomsbury Books
London

Carol Brendlinger and Michael Wild

Menu 1
(*Left*)
Open-Faced Goat Cheese Tart
Swordfish with
Spicy Tomato-Orange Sauce

As a girl, Carol Brendlinger cooked for her six younger children, but she never thought about being a chef until she got her first job – cooking three meals a day for 110 people at a camp in the middle of the Arizona desert. After this rugged yet enjoyable apprenticeship, she returned to San Francisco and worked her way up from salad chef to head chef in local restaurants.

For Michael Wild, his French mother and his own extensive travels were his culinary inspiration. 'My mother cooked anywhere with whatever was at hand. So, I learned to shop and cook anywhere, too,' he says. Today, wherever he goes, he seeks out 'real' cooking.

Though their backgrounds differ sharply, Carol Brendlinger and Michael Wild have developed compatible cooking styles. For these menus, they utilize foods commonly associated with certain regions of France and combine them with some unexpected ingredients.

Menu 1, for example, calls for a number of ingredients characteristic of Provençal cooking – garlic, olive oil, fresh herbs, anchovies, and tomatoes. The cooks add goat cheese, Greek olives, and chili peppers to come up with their unusual appetizer and swordfish entrée.

For their hearty Menu 2 dinner from Alsace, they offer such typical dishes as garlic sausages and red cabbage simmered with Alsatian Riesling, but add surprises such as hazelnuts, juniper berries, and fresh ginger to the sausage, and raspberry vinegar to the salad dressing.

Menu 3 is more traditional. Here they use buckwheat flour, scallops, apples. cider, lamb, cream, butter, and Calvados to create a meal that you might find any day in Brittany.

A fluted tart filled with goat cheese, Greek olives, red pepper, red onion, and anchovies makes an unusual first course. The entrée of swordfish steaks is served with a herb- and chili-enhanced tomato sauce and is garnished with orange sections and chopped scallions.

Open-Faced Goat Cheese Tart
Swordfish with Spicy Tomato-Orange Sauce

The dramatic, colourful goat cheese tart calls for several unusual ingredients. The crust contains polenta, a type of cornmeal used as a staple in Italy. For the tart's topping, select a fresh mild-flavoured goat cheese, such as Montrachet. Or, if you prefer, combine feta cheese with cream cheese. Kalamata olives are juicy, slightly bitter purple-black Greek olives cured in vinegar.

Swordfish is a firm-textured oily fish. If it is unavailable, suitable substitutes are shark, tuna, or any other firm, white fish.

What to drink

These provençal flavours will match a full-bodied, dry white wine from the Rhône Valley such as a white Châteauneuf-du-Pape or Crozes-Hermitages.

Start-to-Finish Steps

1   Prepare onions, garlic, scallions, and mixed herbs for tart and swordfish recipes.
2   Follow tart recipe steps 1 to 6.
3   Remove crust from oven and follow swordfish recipe steps 1 to 4.
4   While sauce is reducing, follow tart recipe steps 7 and 8.
5   While tart is baking, follow swordfish recipe step 5.
6   When tart is done, follow swordfish recipe step 6 and serve tart as first course.
7   Follow swordfish recipe steps 7 to 10 and serve.

Open-Faced Goat Cheese Tart

The crust:
60 g (2 oz) coarse polenta or coarse cornmeal
125 g (4 oz) flour
Pinch of salt
60 ml (2 fl oz) olive oil

The topping:
250 g (½ lb) goat cheese
125 ml (4 fl oz) heavy cream
15 g (½ oz) minced mixed herbs
2 cloves garlic, peeled and minced
10 to 15 Kalamata olives or pitted black olives
1 red bell pepper
½ small red onion, peeled and thinly sliced
6 scallion tops, thinly sliced
10 anchovy fillets, soaked in cold water to remove salt, if desired

1   Preheat oven to 230°C (450°F or Mark 8).
2   For crust, combine dry ingredients in large bowl. Add olive oil and stir until blended. Add 60 ml (2 fl oz) cold water. The dough will be very firm. If crumbly, add 1 tablespoon water to make dough stick together.
3   Press dough firmly and evenly in 22 cm (9 inch) tart pan. Prick bottom of crust with fork.
4   Bake crust until edges are slightly browned, 10 to 15 minutes. Transfer pan to rack to cool.
5   While crust is baking, make filling: Pit olives, if using Kalamatas, and slice thinly. Wash bell pepper and pat dry. Halve, core, and seed pepper; cut half of pepper into dice.
6   In large bowl, beat goat cheese, cream, herbs, and garlic into a thick paste.
7   Spread mixture over crust. Arrange olives, bell pepper, onion, scallions, and anchovies in circles on top.
8   Bake 10 minutes, or just until heated through. Serve as soon as possible so that crust does not become soggy.

Swordfish with Spicy Tomato-Orange Sauce

3 medium-size ripe tomatoes
2 fresh medium-hot chilies, or 1 teaspoon to
  1 tablespoon red pepper flakes
2 oranges
1 lemon
125 ml (4 fl oz) olive oil
Small red onion, peeled and finely chopped
3 cloves garlic, peeled and minced
2 level tablespoons minced mixed herbs
125 ml (4 fl oz) dry white wine or dry vermouth
Four 1 to 1½ cm (½ to ¾ inch) thick swordfish
  steaks
Salt and freshly ground black pepper
2 to 3 chopped scallions for garnish

1 Peel, seed, and chop tomatoes. If using fresh chilies, rinse and pat dry. Split in half lengthwise and remove membranes and seeds. Cut into small dice.
2 Peel 1 orange and cut into sections. Squeeze juice from lemon and remaining orange.
3 In large skillet, heat 60 ml (2 fl oz) olive oil over medium heat. Add onion, chilies, garlic, and herbs, and sauté, stirring with wooden spoon, until soft, about 5 minutes.
4 Add wine and fruit juices, increase heat to high, and boil briskly until reduced to a syrup, 4 to 6 minutes.
5 Add tomatoes and cook just until heated through, 1 minute. Season with salt and pepper to taste, cover, and remove pan from heat.
6 Preheat grill. Arrange steaks on grill pan and brush each with 1 tablespoon of olive oil.
7 Grill swordfish 5 to 7½ cm (2 to 3 inches) from heating element, about 5 minutes per side (depending on thickness), until almost opaque. Turn steaks carefully using metal spatula.
8 While fish is grilling, reheat sauce, if necessary.
9 Spoon some sauce onto heatproof serving platter and arrange fish on top. Spoon more sauce over fish and garnish with orange sections and scallions.
10 Set platter under grill to heat oranges and allow fish to finish cooking, about 2 minutes. Serve immediately.

Added touch
Although this puffy, light dessert requires lengthy preparation, the results are worth the effort. Brandy-flavoured crêpes form the crust of the apricot-flavoured soufflé, and puréed apricots that have been simmered in white wine make up the sauce. Save the extra two or three leftover crêpes for a snack.

Apricot Soufflé Crêpes

The sauce:
125 g (¼ lb) dried apricots
750 ml (1½ pts) dry white wine, approximately

The crêpes:
125 g (4 oz) flour, approximately
2 eggs
175 ml (4 fl oz) half-and-half or light cream
1 tablespoon Calvados or brandy
2 level tablespoons sugar
Pinch of salt
2 level tablespoons unsalted butter, melted

The soufflé
2 eggs
60 g (2 oz) sugar

1 For the sauce, combine apricots and 500 ml (1 pt) wine in small saucepan and bring to a boil over high heat. Lower heat and simmer 20 minutes.
2 Transfer apricots and wine to food processor or food mill and purée. Set aside.
3 For the crêpes, combine crêpe ingredients in large mixing bowl, using only enough flour to make a slightly runny batter.
4 Place a small well-seasoned or non-stick skillet over medium-high heat. Add a few tablespoons of batter, tilting and turning the skillet so batter covers bottom evenly, and cook 1 to 2 minutes, or until lightly coloured. Turn crêpe and cook another 30 seconds. Turn crêpe out onto wax paper. Cover with another sheet of waxed paper. Repeat with remaining batter. There should be enough batter for 6 or 7 crêpes.
5 Butter four 10 to 12½ cm (4 to 5 inch) tart moulds. Fit 1 crêpe into each; the edges should stick out in folds.
6 For soufflé, preheat oven to 190°C (375°F or Mark 5). Separate eggs. In large bowl, beat whites with electric mixer at high speed until stiff. Add sugar and beat another minute.
7 In small bowl, mix yolks with 100 ml (3 fl oz) reserved apricot purée. Stir in a spoonful of whites to lighten yolk mixture. With rubber spatula, gently fold yolk mixture into whites just until incorporated.
8 Divide soufflé mixture among the 4 'moulded' crêpes. Bake 15 to 20 minutes, until puffed and brown. Transfer to a rack.
9 In small saucepan, heat remaining apricot purée, adding enough wine to make a thin sauce.
10 Spoon sauce around edges of 4 plates. Tilting mould, gently nudge each soufflé out into centre of plate. Drizzle with additional sauce and serve.

The sausages, made of ground pork, duck, and veal, are seasoned with an unusual combination of hazelnuts, juniper berries, and ginger. If desired, a natural casing for these patties can be formed with caul fat, bought in sheets from your butcher.

What to drink

This Alsatian meal demands a wine from its native region: an Alsatian Riesling or a Sylvaner.

The vivid colours of the salad and the main course make this a festive meal. Arrange the sausage patties, garnished with watercress, on a bed of the baked cabbage, and serve the creamy juniper berry sauce for the sausages on the side.

Start-to-Finish Steps

1 For sausages and sauce recipes, toast juniper berries in small, dry sauté pan until firm and puffed, 3 to 4 minutes. Juice lemons for cabbage, sauce, and salad recipes.
2 Follow cabbage recipe steps 1 to 3.
3 Follow sausages recipe steps 1 to 10.
4 Follow salad recipe step 1.
5 Follow sauce recipe steps 1 and 2.
6 While sauce is reducing, follow salad recipe steps 2 to 5.
7 Follow sauce recipe steps 3 and 4.
8 Follow salad recipe steps 6 and 7, sausages recipe step 11, sauce recipe step 5, and serve.

Garlic Sausages with Red Cabbage

1 kg (2 lbs) uncooked meat, not minced (a mixture of pork, duck, and veal or two combined)
60 g (2 oz) hazelnuts
250 g (½ lb) caul fat (optional)
4 shallots
6 cloves garlic
1 tablespoon juniper berries, toasted
5 cm (2 inch) piece fresh ginger
1 teaspoon salt
2 apples. preferably Granny Smith or Pippin (about 350 g (¾ lb) total weight)
Freshly ground black pepper
Red cabbage (see following recipe)
Watercress sprigs for garnish (optional)

1 Preheat oven to 190°C (375°F or Mark 5).
2 In food processor fitted with metal blade or with mincer, mince meats until fairly smooth. Transfer to large bowl and set aside. Rinse out processor bowl.

3 Arrange hazelnuts in a single layer on baking sheet and toast in oven until light brown, about 12 minutes. Remove nuts from oven and rub with paper towels to remove skins. Set aside.
4 If using caul fat, soak in large bowl of cold water at least 10 minutes.
5 Peel shallots and garlic. In food processor or with chef's knife, mince shallots, garlic, juniper berries, and ginger with 1 teaspoon salt. Add to meat.
6 In processor or or with chef's knife, coarsely chop hazelnuts and add to meat mixture.
7 If desired, peel apples; halve and core. In processor fitted with shredding disc or with grater, shred apples.
8 Add apples and pepper to taste to meat mixture, and mix well with your hands.
9 Drain caul fat and pat dry. Using about 100 g (3 oz) for each sausage, form mixture into patties and wrap in caul fat, if using.

10 Place patties on top of red cabbage mixture and bake 30 minutes, until lightly golden.

11 Divide cabbage among 4 large plates. Place 2 sausage patties on each plate and garnish with watercress sprigs, if desired.

Red Cabbage

Medium-size red onion
1/2 head red cabbage (about 625 g (1 1/4 lb))
3 apples, preferably Granny Smith or Pippin (about 625 g (1 1/4 lb) total weight)
Juice of 2 lemons (about 125 ml (4 fl oz))
250 ml (8 fl oz) dry white wine, preferably Riesling

1 Peel onion. In food processor fitted with slicing disc or with chef's knife, thinly slice cabbage and onion, and transfer to large baking dish.

2 If desired, peel apples; halve and core. In food processor fitted with shredding disc or with grater, grate apples. Transfer apples to large bowl and toss with lemon juice and wine.

3 Turn mixture into baking dish and toss with cabbage and onion. Set aside.

Juniper Berry Sauce

3/4 ltr (1 pt) heavy cream
2 tablespoons juniper berries, toasted
2 1/2 cm (1 inch) piece fresh ginger
2 shallots
500 ml (1 pt) dry white wine, preferably Riesling
Juice of 1 lemon (about 60 ml (2 fl oz))
Salt and freshly ground black pepper

1 In medium-size non-aluminium saucepan, combine cream, juniper berries, and ginger, and cook slowly over low heat until cream has reduced to 250 ml (8 fl oz), 15 to 20 minutes.

2 While cream is reducing, peel and mince shallots. In small saucepan, combine shallots, wine, and lemon juice, and cook over medium-high heat until liquid has reduced to 125 ml (4 fl oz), about 10 minutes.

3 Lower heat to medium and stir in wine mixture.

4 Remove ginger, and season sauce with salt and pepper to taste. Remove pan from heat, cover, and keep warm.

5 Transfer sauce to sauceboat or small bowl.

Cucumber, Beet, and Onion Salad

3 young beets (about 250 g (1/2 lb) total weight)
175 ml (6 fl oz) raspberry vinegar
Juice of 2 lemons (about 125 ml (4 fl oz))
2 1/2 teaspoons salt
Freshly ground black pepper
2 level tablespoons sugar (optional)
Large cucumber, or 2 small cucumbers
Medium-size red onion
Large bunch watercress
Small bunch chives
2 tablespoons olive oil

1 Peel beets. In food processor fitted with metal blade or with grater, grate beets. In small bowl, combine beets with 125 ml (4 fl oz) raspberry vinegar, 2 tablespoons lemon juice, 1 teaspoon salt, and pepper to taste. Check seasoning: If beets are not sweet, add 1 level tablespoon sugar.

2 Peel cucumber, halve lengthwise, and, using teaspoon, seed, if necessary. Cut cucumber on diagonal into 2 1/2 mm (1/8 inch) thick slices. In another small bowl, combine cucumber with 60 ml (2 fl oz) lemon juice, 1 1/2 teaspoons salt, pepper to taste, and remaining sugar.

3 Peel onion and cut into 2 1/2 mm (1/8 inch) thick slices. In small bowl, combine onion with 500 ml (1 pt) cold water and remaining 60 ml (2 fl oz) raspberry vinegar.

4 Wash watercress and dry in salad spinner or pat dry with paper towels. Remove tough stems and discard. Wrap watercress in paper towels and refrigerate until ready to serve.

5 Wash chives and pat dry with paper towels. Chop coarsely and set aside.

6 Just before serving, place watercress in medium-size bowl and toss with olive oil.

7 Drain vegetables and pat dry with paper towels. Arrange vegetables and watercress in concentric circles on salad plates and sprinkle with chives.

Crêpes with Scallops and Calvados Beurre Blanc
Grilled Lamb Chops with Parsley Butter
Green Beans and Carrots in Garlic-Cream Sauce

Buckwheat crêpes topped with scallops in butter sauce can precede the thick lamb chops and julienne carrots and beans.

Buckwheat crêpes, scallops, and _beurre blanc_, here united for a rich first course, are quite essential elements of Brittany's cuisine. In particular, buckwheat flour is a staple ingredient that appears in many Breton dishes. Because buckwheat flour has a strong nutlike flavour, most recipes, including this one, call for combining it with wheat flour for a milder taste. For this recipe, the buckwheat flour should not be sifted. Buy it at health food stores or speciality food shops and store it in an airtight container in a cool, dry place.

This unusual version of the classic _beurre blanc_, or white butter sauce, typically served with seafood, is an emulsion of wine, Calvados, apple juice, minced shallot, and chilled butter.. The _buerre blanc_ remains creamy during cooking because you add the butter slowly while stirring over low heat to keep the sauce from boiling. Too much heat causes the sauce to separate. Calvados, a dry apple brandy distilled from apple cider, is named after an area bordering the English Channel in Normandy. Aged Calvados is best for drinking, but an immature Calvados will do for cooking, giving sauces a mild apple flavour. Most supermarkets sell Calvados, but apple-flavoured brandies are acceptable substitutes.

What to drink

If you can find good, dry cider, try it with this Breton menu. A simple, crisp white wine, such as a French Muscadet or Italian Verdicchio, would taste fine with the first course. The cook suggesets an older California Cabernet or Pinot Noir for the grilled lamb, but a good Saint-Émilion would serve equally well. If you're feeling truly Breton, have a small glass of Calvados after your dessert as a *digestif*.

Start-to-Finish Steps

1 Juice lemons for beurre blanc and lamb chops recipes. Follow beurre blanc recipe steps 1 and 2.
2 Follow crêpes recipe step 1.
3 Follow lamb chops recipe steps 1 and 2.
4 Follow green beans recipe steps 1 and 2.
5 Follow scallops recipe steps 1 to 3.
6 Follow crêpes recipe step 3.
7 Follow beurre blanc recipe step 3.
8 Follow lamb chops recipe step 3, scallops recipe step 4 to 7, and serve with crêpes for first course.
9 Follow green beans recipe step 3 and lamb chops recipe steps 4 and 5.
10 Follow green beans recipe step 4, lamb chops recipe step 6, and serve.

Crêpes with Scallops and Calvados Beurre Blanc

1 green apple
1 bunch chives
1 red bell pepper
2 level tablespoons unsalted butter
250 g (½ lb) bay scallops
Salt
Freshly ground black pepper
Crêpes (see following recipe)
Calvados Beurre Blanc (see following recipe)

1 Preheat oven to 130°C (250°F or Mark 1).
2 Halve, core, and dice apple. Wash chives and pat dry with paper towels; finely chop enough to meaure 2 tablespoons. Rinse bell pepper and pat dry with paper towels. Halve, core, and seed pepper; dice enough to measure 60 g (2 oz).
3 Place 4 dinner plates in oven to warm.
4 In large sauté pan, melt butter over medium heat. Add apple and pepper, cook, stirring occasionally, 2 minutes.
5 Add scallops and cook, stirring 2 minutes.

6 Season to taste with salt and pepper and add chives.
7 Divide crêpes equally among 4 warm plates. Spoon scallop mixture over crêpes and top each serving with beurre blanc.

Crêpes

1 level tablespoon unsalted butter
30 g (1 oz) buckwheat flour
60 g (2 oz) plain flour
1 egg
1 tablespoon Calvados
Pinch of salt

1 In small heavy-gauge saucepan or butter warmer, melt butter.
2 In small bowl, combine all ingredients, including butter.
3 Lightly butter griddle or large skillet and place over medium heat. Drop batter by tablespoonfuls to make 7½ cm (3 inch) pancakes. Cook about 30 seconds per side, or until lightly browned. As crêpes are cooked, transfer them to heatproof platter and keep warm in oven until ready to serve. Repeat with remaining batter; you will have about 20 crêpes.

Calvados Buerre Blanc

1 shallot
250 ml (8 fl oz) dry white wine
125 ml (4 fl oz) unfiltered apple juice
60 ml (2 fl oz) Calvados
Juice of 2 lemons (about 60 ml (2 fl oz))
250 g (4 oz) unsalted butter, chilled
Salt
Freshly ground pepper

1 Peel and mince shallot.
2 In small saucepan, combine wine, apple juice, Calvados, lemon juice, and shallot. Simmer mixture gently over low heat until reduced to a syrupy glaze, about 30 minutes.
3 Cut butter into tablespoon-size pieces and add to glaze, 1 tablespoon at a time, stirring until each piece is incorporated before adding next. Keep sauce on heat just until barely warm and last piece of butter has melted or sauce will separate. Add salt and pepper to taste.

Grilled Lamb Chops with Parsely Butter

1 bunch parsley
2 cloves garlic
1 shallot
1 teaspoon salt
5 level tablespoons unsalted butter, at room temperature
Juice of 1 lemon (about 60 ml (2 fl oz))
Four 5 cm (2 inch) thick lamb chops (about 1 kg (2 lbs) total weight)
60 ml (2 fl oz) heavy cream

1 Peel garlic and shallot. In food processor or with chef's knife, chop parsley, garlic, shallot, and salt.
2 In small bowl, blend parsley mixture with butter and lemon juice. Set aside.
3 Preheat grill.
4 Trim fat off lamb chops and discard. Arrange chops in single layer on grill pan and top each with ¹/₂ tablespoon of cream. Grill 7¹/₂ to 10 cm (3 to 4 inches) from heating element, 6 minutes for rare, 8 minutes for medium, or 10 minutes for well done.
5 Turn chops and top each with another spoonful of cream. Continue grilling another 6 to 10 minutes.
6 Transfer chops to heatproof serving platter and top each with a spoonful of parsley butter. Place platter under grill 1 minute to melt butter. Transfer chops to individual plates.

Green Beans and Carrots in Garlic-Cream Sauce

250 g (¹/₂ lb) green beans
Large carrot (about 125 g (¹/₄ lb))
2 cloves garlic
250 ml (8 fl oz) heavy cream
Salt
Freshly ground pepper

1 Remove stem ends from beans. Wash beans, pat dry with paper towels, and cut into julienne.
2 Peel carrot and cut into 5 cm (2 inch) long pieces. Halve each piece lengthwise and cut into julienne. Peel garlic.
3 In small saucepan, combine green beans, carrot, garlic, cream, and salt and pepper to taste, and bring to a boil over high heat. Reduce heat to low and simmer 10 minutes, or until vegetables are crisp-tender.
4 Remove and discard garlic cloves, and turn vegetables into serving bowl.

Added touch
Madeleines are small sweet cakes baked in a madeleine mould, which has indentations shaped like elongated scallop shells. Here the madeleines are flavoured with orange-flower water, a fragrant liquid made from distilled orange blossoms. Chemists usually stock orange-flower water.

Madeleines

125 g (4 oz) plus 2 level tablespoons unsalted butter
1 lime
1 lemon
3 eggs
150 g (5 oz) sugar
¹/₂ teaspoon vanilla extract
1 tablespoon orange-flower water, or grazed zest of ¹/₂ orange
125 g (4 oz) plus 1 level tablespoon plain flour
¹/₂ teaspoon baking powder

1 In small heavy-gauge saucepan or butter warmer, melt butter over low heat. Set aside to cool.
2 Grate zest from lemon and lime, and squeeze enough lemon to measure 1 tablespoon juice.
3 In large bowl, combine eggs and sugar, and beat with electric mixer until almost stiff.
4 Add lemon and lime zest, lemon juice, vanilla extract, and orange-flower water, and beat a few more minutes, until well blended.
5 Sift together 125 g (4 oz) of flour and baking powder. Using rubber spatula, gently fold into batter. Stir in 125 g (4 oz) of melted butter.
6 Set the batter aside to rest in a cool place at least 15 minutes or up to 2 hours.
7 Meanwhile, preheat oven to 180°C (350°F or Mark 4).
8 In small bowl, combine remaining melted butter with remaining flour. Brush madeleine moulds with mixture. Add enough batter to fill each mould two thirds full.
9 Bake 10 to 15 minutes, or until madeleines are slightly browned at the edges. Transfer to a rack to cool.

Jeanne Voltz

Menu 1
(*Right*)
Carrot Soup
Boeuf Bourguignon Sauté
Butter-Braised Broccoli

All her life, food writer Jeanne Voltz has been a Francophile. As a girl, she envied the American literary figures who lived in Paris; Hemingway, the Fitzgeralds, Gertrude Stein. Daily, they sampled the cuisine she could only read about in novels. When she finally visited France as an adult, she 'could hardly taste fast enough or eat enough' to satisfy her curiosity and long-time envy. Nothing had prepared her for the excitement of the exquisite foods she ate.

Jeanne Voltz has made many pilgrimages to France and found it difficult to decide which of her favourite dishes to present here. Her Menu 1, a hearty family meal, features a full-flavoured carrot soup, *boeuf bourguignon*, the renowned main dish from Burgundy, and butter-braised broccoli. The beef entrée is normally slow-cooked (3 to 4 hours), but this version calls for a tender cut of beef, cubed for quick sautéing.

In Menu 2, two recipes are reminiscent of Bordeaux – poussins in red wine and cauliflower au gratin. The warm chicken liver salad is a variation on a recipe from nearby Gascony, where warm *foie gras* is a prelude to many meals.

Menu 3 features grilled butterflied leg of lamb, mushrooms stuffed with snail butter (which contains no snails but is so-called because it is always used to fill *escargots à la bourguignonne*), and roasted potatoes.

Colourful carrot soup precedes the main course of tender beef, browned bacon, carrots, and mushrooms in red wine suce. For maximum ease, serve the sauté on a large platter and let your guests help themselves. Crisp broccoli completes the meal.

Carrot soup
Boeuf Bourguignon Sauté
Butter-Braised Broccoli

French thrift has inspired some of the world's great soups. This one is best prepared with large mature carrots, sometimes called 'cooking' carrots, which have a rich flavour. If you can find only slender young carrots, use one or two extra, and accent their flavour with a pinch or two of sugar.

Selecting beautiful broccoli is simple: Look for firm, bright green heads with compact buds. Avoid any that have yellowed – a sure sign of age. Refrigerate unwashed broccoli in a plastic bag. It will keep for several days.

What to drink

The right drink here is a medium-bodied red wine from southern Burgundy – a Mercurey, for instance, or a Beaujolais Villages. A California, Washington, or Oregon Pinot Noir would also make a fine accompaniment.

Start-to-Finish Steps

1 Follow beef recipe steps 1 to 4 and soup recipe steps 1 to 5.
2 Follow beef recipe step 5 and broccoli recipe step 1.
3 Follow soup recipe steps 6 and 7, and broccoli recipe step 2.
4 While broccoli is braising, follow beef recipe step 6 and then broccoli recipe step 3.
5 Follow beef recipe steps 7 and 8, and broccoli recipe step 4.
6 Follow soup recipe steps 8 and 9, and beef recipe step 9.
7 Follow soup recipe step 10 and serve.
8 Follow beef recipe step 10 and serve with broccoli.

Carrot Soup

Small yellow onion
1 stalk celery
2 large 'cooking' carrots or 4 small young carrots
Small russet or new potato
2 level tablespoons unsalted butter
Whole nutmeg, preferably, or $1/2$ teaspoon ground
1 teaspoon salt
Freshly ground white pepper
300 ml (10 fl oz) heavy cream, approximately

1 Preheat oven to SLOW.
2 Peel and thinly slice enough onion to measure about 45 g ($1^1/_2$ oz). Wash, trim, and thinly slice celery. Peel and thinly slice carrots and potato.
3 In large saucepan, melt butter over medium heat. Add onion and celery, and cook, stirring occasionally, until onion is tender but not browned, 3 to 5 minutes.
4 Grate enough nutmeg to measure $1/2$ teaspoon, if using whole.
5 Add carrots, potato, salt, $1/4$ teaspoon nutmeg, pepper to taste, and 750 ml ($1^1/_2$ pts) water. Cover saucepan and bring to a boil over high heat. Reduce heat to low and simmer 8 to 10 minutes, or until carrots and potato are soft.
6 Place 4 bowls or soup plates in oven to warm.
7 Remove pan from heat, uncover, and allow vegetables to cool slightly.
8 Coarsely purée vegetables and liquid, in batches if necessary, in food processor or blender.
9 Return soup to saucepan and stir in cream, thinning to desired consistency. Reheat soup over low heat, and add additional salt, pepper, or nutmeg to taste.
10 Ladle soup into warmed bowls and serve.

Boeuf Bourguignon Sauté

Large yellow onion
Small bunch shallots
250 g ($1/2$ lb) slab bacon
2 small carrots
12 small mushrooms
750 g ($1^1/_2$ lbs) boneless top sirloin steak or tenderloin, cut into 4 cm ($1^1/_2$ inch) cubes
1 bay leaf
1 teaspoon thyme, crumbled
150 ml (5 fl oz) dry red wine, approximately
Salt and freshly ground black pepper
Small bunch parsley for garnish (optional)

1 Peel and chop onion. Peel and mince enough shallots to measure 30 g (1 oz). Cut bacon into $2^1/_2$ cm (1 inch) squares.
2 In large, wide saucepan or sauté pan, cook bacon over medium heat until pan is well coated with fat. Add onion and shallots, and cook until bacon is

almost crisp and onion is tender but not browned, about 5 minutes.

3 While bacon is cooking, peel carrots and cut into 5 cm (2 inch) lengths. Wipe mushrooms clean with damp paper towels; set aside.

4 Add carrots and beef to pan, and cook over medium-high heat, stirring occasionally, until meat is evenly browned, about 10 minutes.

5 When beef is browned, add bay leaf, thyme, wine, and salt and pepper to taste. Cover and simmer over low heat 10 to 12 minutes, until fragrant.

6 Wash parsley, if using, and pat dry. Chop enough to measure 1 tablespoon; set aside.

7 Add additional wine, if needed to keep meat moist, and gently stir in mushrooms. Cover and cook over low heat 5 minutes. Meat will be medium-rare to rare and carrots crisp-tender. Do *not* overcook meat.

8 Place serving platter in oven to warm.

9 Remove and discard bay leaf. With a spoon or bulb baster, skim off any visible fat. Remove sauté pan from heat and keep covered until ready to serve.

10 When ready to serve, turn beef and vegetables onto warm platter and serve garnished with chopped parsley, if desired.

Butter-Braised Broccoli

2 bunches broccoli (about 750 g (1¹/₂ lbs) total
   weight)
3 level tablespoons unsalted butter
Salt and freshly ground white pepper

1 Wash broccoli and do *not* dry. Cut off the florets, or flowery heads, leaving 2¹/₂ cm (1 inch) or so of stem intact.

2 Place florets in large saucepan over medium heat. Add butter, cover, and braise 5 minutes in the water remaining on florets after washing, checking to see if broccoli is beginning to brown and adding

1 to 2 tablespoons water, if necessary. Sprinkle lightly with salt and pepper.

3 Reduce heat, cover, and continue cooking until broccoli is crisp yet tender, about 3 minutes longer.

4 Turn into heatproof serving bowl and keep warm in oven until ready to serve.

Added touch

For this elegant dessert, choose the pear variety that suits your palate: Bell-shaped Bartletts have a mildly sweet flavour; plump Anjous are rich and spicy; and slender Boscs are usually slightly acidic.

Pears Poached in Vanilla Syrup

175 g (6 oz) sugar
1 teaspoon vanilla extract
4 Bartlett, Anjou, or Bosc pears
125 ml (4 fl oz) crème fraîche

1 In large skillet, bring 500 ml (1 pt) water and sugar to a boil over high heat, stirring until sugar is dissolved. Boil 2 minutes, add vanilla extract, and keep syrup at boiling point.

2 One at a time, peel pears and core from bottom, leaving stems intact. (It is almost impossible to remove the complete core, but use a sharp knife or apple corer to scoop out as much of it as possible). If necessary, trim bottoms of pears flat, so they will stand frimly upright.

3 Using tongs, dip each pear in boiling syrup to coat well and prevent darkening, and turn pear on its side in syrup.

4 After all pears have been added to skillet, test the first one for doneness by piercing it with the tip of a small knife or a skewer. If tender, remove with tongs, holding briefly over skillet to drain. As each pear is done, remove from syrup, drain, and place upright in serving dish.

5 Raise heat under skillet to high and cook syrup until reduced by half, about 15 minutes. Pour syrup around pears in serving dish, cover loosely with foil or plastic wrap, and refrigerate at least 30 minutes or until ready to serve.

6 Divide cold pears among individual dessert plates and serve topped with a generous spoonful of crème fraîche.

Leftover suggestion

Peel leftover broccoli stems and slice them thinly for stir-frying or to use as a garnish for soups or salads. Also, steamed, peeled, and diced broccoli stems are a delicious addition to omelettes and quiches.

Chicken Liver and Lettuce Salad
Poussins in Claret
Cauliflower au Gratin

Serve the chicken liver salad before or with the main course of poussins and cauliflower au gratin.

The first-course salad is an adaptation of a Gascon dish that calls for warm goose or duck livers. For her version, Jeanne Voltz uses chicken livers, cooked briefly so they remain tender and juicy. Instead of Romaine, you may want to try radicchio or arugula. For a more highly seasoned salad, add minced garlic to taste.

The red Bordeaux used in the sauce for the poussins is called claret – the traditional English name for the light red wines of Bordeaux.

What to drink

This menu is ideal for either light red or big white wines. For red, choose a Bordeaux wine, such as a Margaux or Saint-Emilion, which you can also use for the sauce for the poussins. For white, a California Chardonnay or a *premier cru* Chablis would be a good choice.

Start-to-Finish Steps

1 Follow poussins recipe steps 1 to 3 and salad recipe steps 1 and 2.
2 Turn poussins and follow cauliflower recipe steps 1 to 4.
3 Follow poussins recipe steps 4 and 5, and cauliflower recipe steps 5 and 6.
4 Check poussins periodically, turning and adjusting heat as needed. Follow salad recipe steps 7 and 8.
5 Follow cauliflower recipe steps 7 and 8.
6 Follow salad recipe steps 5 to 7, poussins recipe step 6, and serve with cauliflower.

Chicken Liver and Lettuce Salad

Small head Bibb or Boston lettuce
8 to 10 large leaves Romaine lettuce
125 g (¼ lb) bacon (approximately 4 slices)
250 g (½ lb) chicken livers
Small yellow onion
2 teaspoons sugar
1 level tablespoon Dijon mustard
2 tablespoons red wine vinegar

1 Wash lettuce thoroughly and dry in salad spinner or pat dry with paper towels. Tear lettuce leaves into bite-size pieces and arrange on individual salad plates. Cover with plastic and refrigerate.
2 Slice bacon into 2½ cm (1 inch) squares and

chicken livers into 2½ cm (1 inch) cubes. Peel and mince onion.
3 In a large heavy-gauge skillet, cook bacon until almost crisp, about 3 minutes.
4 While bacon is cooking, rinse chicken livers under cold running water and pat dry with paper towels. Remove membranes; set aside.
5 Add onion and chicken livers, and cook, stirring often, until livers are browned but still tender, about 4 minutes.
6 Add sugar and mustard, and stir well. Add vinegar, carefully pouring it down side of skillet to avoid splattering, and cook mixture, stirring, about 2 minutes, or until bubbly.
7 Divide liver mixture among salad plates and top with sauce. Serve while still warm.

Poussins in Claret

2 poussins (about 625 g (1¼ lbs) each), with backbone removed, split, and flattened
250 g (½ lb) medium-size mushrooms
2 level tablespoons unsalted butter
1 tablespoon olive oil
½ teaspoon dried thyme
1 teaspoon salt
Freshly ground black pepper
125 ml (4 fl oz) Margaux or other red Bordeaux wine

1 In a few minutes you can easily bone, split, and flatten poussins yourself. Remove giblets and necks from poussins, and refrigerate for another use. With poultry shears, cut down each side of backbone from tail to neck, splitting poussin in half; discard backbone. Flatten halves of poussins on countertop or cutting board and, with paring knife, cut through breast, slit membrane over breast bone, and remove it. With the heel of your hand, press halves flat again.
2 Wipe mushrooms clean with damp towels; set aside.
3 In 1 or 2 large heavy-gauge skillets, melt butter with oil over medium-high heat. With skin sides down, sauté poussins until golden, about 5 minutes. Turn and sauté another 5 minutes,
4 Sprinkle with thyme, salt, and pepper to taste. Add mushrooms to skillet, and stir until thoroughly coated with pan juices.
5 Add wine and cook 15 to 25 minutes, or until liquid is almost absorbed and poussins are tender but not dry.
6 Divide poussins among individual plates and top with pan juices and mushrooms.

Cauliflower au Gratin

Large head cauliflower (about 750 g (1¹/₂ lbs))
¹/₂ teaspoon salt
1 slice stale white bread
60 g (2 oz) Gruyère cheese
60 g (2 oz) Parmesan cheese
125 ml (4 fl oz) heavy cream
Freshly ground white pepper

1   Preheat oven to 230°C (450°F or Mark 8). Generously butter shallow rectangular baking dish.
2   Cut off leaves and remove core from cauliflower. Break or cut head into small florets; reserve core and leaves for another use.
3   In large saucepan, combine florets, salt, and 125 ml (4 fl oz) water and bring to a boil over high heat. Reduce heat to medium and cook, covered, until crisp-tender, about 7 minutes. Check cauliflower and add more hot water, if needed, to prevent burning.
4   In food processor or blender, finely grind the stale bread. Measure out 2 tablespoons of crumbs, place in small bowl, and set aside.
5   In food processor or with grater, shred enough Gruyère to measure 30 g (1 oz) and grate enough Parmesan to measure 2 tablespoons. Combine Parmesan and bread crumbs.
6   Transfer cauliflower to colander, refresh under cold running water, and drain.
7   Arrange cauliflower, with florets facing up, in baking dish. Sprinkle with Gruyère, carefully drizzle with cream, and season with white pepper to taste. Sprinkle evenly with bread crumb-Parmesan mixture.
8   Place dish on top rack of oven and bake about 10 minutes, or until sauce is bubbly and top is lightly browned.

Added touch

Vanilla sugar, prepared in advance and kept as a kitchen staple, imparts a delicious flavour when used in cooking desserts or when sprinkled on fresh fruits. Spoon about 400 g (14 oz) of confectioners' sugar (or granulated sugar, if preferred) into a 1¹/₄ ltr (2 pt) jar with screw-top lid. Push a vanilla bean into the sugar, breaking bean, if necessary, to fit in jar. Cover and let stand at room temperature about three weeks before using. Replenish by adding more sugar as long as vanilla bean retains its flavour.

Caramel Apples with Vanilla Cream

3 level tablespoons lightly salted butter
4 to 6 apples, such as Golden Delicious, Granny Smith, or McIntosh (about 750 g to 1kg (1¹/₂ to 2 lbs) total weight)
100 g (3 oz) sugar, approximately
2 tablespoons brandy, Calvados, or Applejack
Vanilla Cream (see following recipe)

1   In large cast-iron skillet, melt butter, tipping skillet to coat evenly. Turn off heat, but leave skillet on burner to keep hot.
2   One at a time, peel, core, and slice enough apples into 5 mm (¹/₄ inch) thick wedges to measure about 625 g (1¹/₄ lb). As they are cut, place apple slices in skillet and turn with metal tongs to coat with butter.
3   When all apples have ben prepared and coated with butter, spread into a thin layer in skillet. Turn heat to high and cook about 4 minutes, or until apples appear tinged with gold, turning gently with a wide spatula once or twice.
4   Sprinkle with sugar to taste, depending on sweetness of apples, and continue cooking until juices running from apples are almost evaporated.
5   Remove skillet from heat and sprinkle apples with brandy. Return skillet to burner, bring liquid to a fast boil, and cook about 3 minutes, or until juices are syrupy but apples still retain their shape.
6   Turn into serving bowl, cover, and let stand at room temperature until ready to serve. Or refrigerate overnight and reheat before serving
7   To serve, divide among dessert bowls and top with Vanilla Cream.

Vanilla Cream

125 ml (4 fl oz) heavy cream
125 ml (4 fl oz) sour cream
1 level tablespoon vanilla sugar, approximately

1   In small bowl, combine heavy cream, sour cream, and vanilla sugar to taste, and stir until blended.
2   Cover and let stand 1 to 2 hours at room temperature, or refrigerate until 30 minutes before serving. Serve at room temperature.

Mushrooms with Snail Butter
Grilled Butterflied Leg of Lamb in Red Wine
Crock-Roasted Potatoes

Grilled butterflied leg of lamb, seasoned with rosemary and red wine is an elegant main dish for a company meal. A 'butterflied' leg has had the bones and fat removed. Its thick parts are cut so that the meat can be opened out as if it were hinged (resembling a butterfly's wings), then the meat is spread out and pounded flat for grilling.

French cooks often roast potatoes on the stove-top in an earthenware crock, but you can use a heavy cast-iron pot instead. Covered tightly, the potatoes cook slowly without liquid, roasting in their own juices. When they are done, a rich potato aroma permeates the kitchen.

What to drink

The Pommard called for in the lamb recipe would be ideal served along with the entrée. As an alternative, you could select a good Saint-Émilion or Médoc from a small château.

Start-to-Finish Steps

1 Peel and mince shallots for mushrooms and for lamb. Peel and mince garlic for mushrooms. Follow lamb recipe step 1.
2 Follow potatoes recipe steps 1 and 2, and mushrooms recipe steps 1 and 2.
3 Follow lamb recipe steps 2 and 3.

Mushrooms filled with snail, or seasoned, butter and roasted potatoes accompany the succulent lamb.

4 Follow potatoes recipe step 3 and mushrooms recipe steps 3 to 5.
5 Follow lamb recipe steps 4 and 5, and mushrooms recipe step 6.
6 Follow lamb recipe steps 6 to 10 and mushrooms recipe step 7.
7 Follow lamb recipe steps 11 and 12, potatoes recipe step 4, and serve with mushrooms.

Mushrooms with Snail Butter

12 large mushrooms (about 350 g (³/₄ lb) total weight)
Large sprig parsley
4 level tablespoons unsalted butter
2 to 3 large shallots
Small clove garlic
60 ml (2 fl oz) chicken stock

1 Wipe mushrooms clean with damp paper towels. Remove stems and reserve for another use. Wash parsley sprig and pat dry. Chop parsley.
2 In small bowl, break up butter with a fork. Sprinkle parsley, shallots, and garlic over butter. Set aside for at least 15 minutes to allow butter to soften and absorb flavours.
3 In small saucepan, heat chicken stock over low heat. Add mushrooms, cover, and simmer 3 to 4 minutes, or until mushrooms are just tender.
4 While mushrooms simmer, rapidly mix butter with seasonings.
5 With tongs, remove mushrooms from stock and place on paper towels to drain.
6 Arrange mushrooms, with gill sides up, in shallow baking pan. Spoon 1 teaspoon seasoned butter into each cap.
7 Grill mushrooms 10 to 12¹/₂ cm (4 to 5 inches) from heating element about 5 minutes, or until butter is bubbly and mushrooms are heated through.

Grilled Butterflied Leg of Lamb in Red Wine

1¹/₄ kg (2¹/₂ lbs) butterflied leg of lamb
250 ml (8 fl oz) dry red wine, such as Pommard or Médoc
2 to 3 large shallots, peeled and minced
2 teaspoons dried rosemary
Salt
Freshly ground pepper
1 teaspoon cornstarch
Fresh rosemary sprigs for garnish (optional)

1 To marinate lamb, place fat side down in large shallow glass or ceramic dish. Pour wine over meat and sprinkle with shallots and dried rosemary. Turn meat and let stand at room temperature 15 to 30 minutes, turning once or twice.
2 Grease tray or rack of grill pan well to facilitate clean-up. Preheat grill.
3 If using rosemary for garnish, wash and pat dry with paper towels.
4 Using tongs, lift lamb from marinade and place fat side up on grill pan or tray rack. Reserve marinade for sauce.
5 Grill lamb 10 to 12¹/₂ cm (4 to 5 inches) from heat element 8 to 10 minutes, or until well browned.
6 Brush meat with marinade, turn, and brush other side. Grill another 10 to 15 minutes, or until well browned. The thick parts should be rare and thinner sections medium to well done.
7 Place platter under hot running water.
8 Dry platter. Transfer lamb to warm platter and cover loosely with foil.
9 Skim most of fat from drippings and pour drippings into small skillet. Add reserved marinade and bring to a boil over high heat. Season with salt and pepper to taste.
10 Place plates under hot running water to warm.
11 Blend cornstarch with 1 tablespoon of water into a paste. Add cornstarch paste to marinade and cook, stirring, 3 to 5 minutes, or until slightly thickened and smooth.
12 Dry plates. Slice lamb and divide among dinner plates. Top with sauce and serve garnished with rosemary sprigs, if desired.

Crock-Roasted Potatoes

8 to 12 small russet potatoes (about 750 g (1¹/₂ lbs) total weight)
2 cloves garlic (optional)

4 level tablespoons unsalted butter (or lightly salted, if preferred)

1 Wash potatoes. In *very heavy*-gauge casserole with *tight-fitting* cover, arrange potatoes in single layer. Place unpeeled garlic in pot. Cover pan, fitting sheet of aluminium foil or cooking parchment between pot and lid, if necessary, to make a very tight seal.

2 Using a heat diffuser or spreader on cooking surface if needed to produce slow, even heat, place pan over very low heat. Cook potatoes, without adding any liquid, 15 minutes.

3 Using a pot holder, lift cover and use metal tongs to turn potatoes. Do not puncture them. Cover and cook until potatoes are very tender, about 30 minutes.

4 Divide among individual plates and dot with butter.

Added touch

For an elegant summer dessert, use fully ripe, juicy, and fragrant freestone peaches. The coarse peach purée gives texture to the dessert. If you cannot find fresh raspberies for the sauce, substitute frozen ones.

Peach Bavarian Cream with Raspberry Sauce

750 g (1½ lbs) peaches or unsweetened frozen peaches, or Bartlett, Bosc, or Anjou pears (about 250 g (8 oz) puréed)
1 tablespoon freshly squeeezed lemon juice
4 egg yolks plus 3 egg whites
1 envelope unflavoured gelatine
100 g (3 oz) sugar, approximately
125 ml (4 fl oz) milk
125 ml (4 fl oz) heavy cream
Raspberry Sauce (see following recipe)

1 In large saucepan, bring 2½ ltrs (4 pts) of water to a boil. Submerge peaches in boiling water and blanch 30 seconds. Drain, peel, pit, and slice peaches.

2 In processor or blender, coarsely purée enough peaches to measure 250 g (8 oz). Immediately stir in lemon juice to prevent discolouration.

3 Separate egg yolks and whites placing yolks in small bowl, 3 whites in a mixing bowl, and reserving 1 egg white for another use.

4 In top of double grill or in bowl that can be fitted over but not sit in a pan of water, combine gelatine, 100 g (3 oz) sugar, egg yolks, and milk. Add more sugar if peaches are not sweet enough.

1. Crack egg against side of bowl.

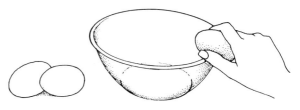

2. Separate each egg by pouring back and forth between halves of shell until the entire white has dropped into one bowl.

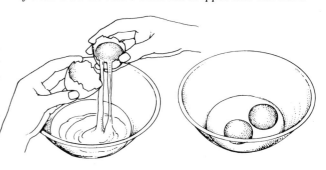

5 Place egg mixture over hot water on very low heat and cook stirring, 3 to 5 minutes, or until thickened and smooth.

6 Cool mixture by setting bowl in large container of cold water for about 15 minutes. Stir in peach purée. Chill in refrigerator until thickened but not set, about 30 minutes.

7 Beat egg whites until stiff but not dry. Fold gently into peach mixture. In another bowl, whip cream and fold into peaches.

8 Rinse a 2 ltr (3 pt) mould in cold water, then turn mixture into mould. Cover and chill overnight or until set, 6 to 8 hours.

9 When ready to serve, unmould Bavarian onto serving plate and top with a few spoonfuls of raspberry sauce. Serve remaining sauce separately.

Raspberry Sauce

500 g (1 lb) fresh raspberries
3 to 4 tablespoons granulated sugar or vanilla sugar
½ teaspoon vanilla extract (omit if using vanilla sugar)

1 Gently rinse raspberries and spread on paper towels to drain.

2 Press raspberries through food mill or strainer set over small bowl to purée pulp and remove seeds.

3 Stir 3 tablespoons sugar and vanilla or vanilla sugar only into purée. Add more sugar to taste. Cover and refrigerate sauce until ready to serve.

Leslee Reis

Menu 1
(*Right*)
Choucroute Salad
Chicken and Sausages in Reisling Sauce
with Egg Noodles

Leslee Reis has travelled often in Alsace and throughout France – but not as an ordinary tourist might. She prefers to visit local farmers, market places, and small unstarred (or perhaps one-starred) restaurants and enjoys observing the terrain and the character of the local people. Her three menus are taken from Alsace and Provence.

Menu 1 is Alsatian. The first-course salad is an adaptation of the famous Alsatian one-course meal *choucroute garnie*, or braised sauerkraut garnished with pieces of pork, salt pork, sausage, or bacon. The entrée also features two other specialities of the region: pork, here in the form of sausages, and Riesling, the celebrated white wine, which is used in the sauce.

Menus 2 and 3 are Provence-inspired. In Menu 2, Leslee Reis has created a fish stew that resembles the *bouillabaisse* of Marseilles. Menu 3 features artichokes braised in olive oil with basil and garlic – a combination typical of the region, as is the union of tomato and garlic, used here for an interesting variation of *coquilles St. Jacques*.

Chicken pieces, sliced garlic sausages, and chopped vegetables are heaped on a bed of golden egg noodles for this Alsatian dinner. For the salad, serve individual portions of sauerkraut on curly lettuce leaves, surrounded by walnuts, cornichons, lardoons, and onions.

Choucroute Salad
Chicken and Sausages in Riesling Sauce
with Egg Noodles

Choucroute, or sauerkraut, a ubiquitous ingredient in Alsatian cooking, is white cabbage that has been finely shredded, salted, and then left to ferment. Pork and mustard are its classic partners; here the cook suggests salt pork and Dijon mustard. The pork is cut into lardoons, or strips, then blanched and fried. Blanching the pork strips tempers their saltiness so that the pork does not overwhelm the onions, walnuts, and *cornichons* (small sour French pickles) in the salad.

Alsatian Riesling, a major flavouring in the sauce for the chicken and sausages, is a dry crisp white wine that complements seafood, poultry, sauerkraut, and pork, and is less sweet than the German or California Rieslings.

What to drink

The cook suggests an Alsatian Riesling or Pinot Blanc to go with the *choucroute* salad in this menu. A New York State, Oregon, or California Riesling would also be good choices.

Start-to-Finish Steps

1 Follow salad recipe step 1.
2 Peel and dice onion. Follow chicken and sausages recipe steps 1 to 5.
3 Follow salad recipe steps 2 to 7.
4 Follow chicken and sausages recipe steps 6 to 8.
5 While water for pasta is coming to a boil, follow salad recipe steps 8 and 9, and serve as first course.
6 Follow chicken and sausages recipe steps 9 and 10, and serve.

Choucroute Salad

250 g (¹/₂ lb) lean salt pork
60 ml (2 fl oz) peanut oil, plus another 5 tablespoons if not using walnut oil
60 g (2 oz) walnut pieces
5 tablespoons walnut oil, preferably, or peanut oil
Salt
300 g (10 oz) sauerkraut, preferably fresh, or prepared
1 head soft lettuce, preferably leaf
60 g (2 oz) cornichons
60 ml (2 fl oz) red wine vinegar
¹/₂ teaspoon Dijon mustard, preferably coarse-grained
¹/₄ teaspoon freshly ground pepper
30 g (1 oz) diced onion

1 Preheat oven to 200°C (400°F or Mark 6).
2 Cut salt pork into lardoons (5 mm thick, 3 cm long (¹/₄ inch thick, 1¹/₂ inch long) julienne). In medium-size saucepan, bring 1¹/₄ ltrs (2 pts) water to a boil over high heat. Add lardoons and blanch 1 minute. Transfer to colander and rinse under cold runnng water. Drain and pat dry with paper towels.
3 In small skillet, heat 2 tablespoons peanut oil over medium heat. Add lardoons and cook, stirring occasionally to prevent burning, 3 to 5 minutes, or until browned. Remove with slotted spoon and drain on paper towels.
4 While lardoons are browning, chop walnuts.
5 In small bowl, mix walnuts with 1 tablespoon walnut or peanut oil and sprinkle with salt to taste. Arrange on cookie sheet in single layer and toast in oven 5 to 8 minutes, or just until brown. Reduce oven temperature to SLOW.
6 While walnuts are toasting, wash lettuce and dry in salad spinner or pat dry with paper towels.

Wrap in paper towels and refrigerate until needed. Cut cornichons into 5 mm (¼ inch) thick slices; set aside.

7 In colander, rinse sauerkraut under cold running water. Drain and pat dry with paper towels. Set aside.

8 For vinaigrette, combine 60 ml (2 fl oz) walnut oil, if using, remaining 2 tablespoons peanut oil (or 6 tablespoons peanut oil if not using walnut oil), vinegar, mustard, ½ teaspoon salt, and pepper in medium-size bowl. Add sauerkraut and toss to coat.

9 Line 4 individual salad bowls with lettuce leaves. Top each with sauerkraut and surround with small portions of lardoons, walnuts, onion, and cornichons.

Chicken and Sausages in Riesling Sauce with Egg Noodles

500 g (1 lb) fresh garlic sausages
1½ kg (3 lb) grilling chicken, cut into 8 pieces
5 tablespoons vegetable oil, approximately
60 g (2 oz) diced onion
2 medium-size carrots
Large turnip
1 celery rib
250 ml (8 fl oz) Alsatian Riesling wine
500 ml (1 pt) chicken stock, preferably homemade
½ teaspoon freshly ground pepper
60 ml (2 fl oz) heavy cream
250 g to 350 g (½ to ¾ lb) 1 cm (½ inch) wide egg noodles, preferably fresh, or dried
1 teaspoon salt

1 Slice sausages into 1 cm (½ inch) thick rounds. Cut rounds into semicircles. In large deep ovenproof skillet, sauté sausages over medium heat only until skins are brown and fat is rendered, about 7 minutes. Remove sausages with slotted spoon and drain on paper towels. Reserve fat in skillet.

2 While sausages are browning, wash chicken pieces and pat dry with paper towels. Add to skillet and sauté over medium heat in sausage fat 5 to 7 minutes, turning to brown evenly to prevent sticking, add 1 to 2 tablespoons vegetable oil. Transfer chicken to platter and set aside.

3 While chicken is browning, peel and dice carrots and turnip. Wash trim, and dice celery.

4 Add onion, carrots, turnip, and celery to skillet, and sauté 2 to 3 minutes, or until soft. If necessary to prevent sticking, add 1 to 2 tablespoons vegetable oil.

5 Return chicken to skillet. Add wine, stock, and pepper, and bring to a boil. Lower heat, cover, and simmer until chicken is tender, 20 to 25 minutes.

6 Return sausages to skillet and simmer another 3 to 4 minutes.

7 Add cream to skillet and stir until blended. Simmer 1 to 2 minutes to marry the flavours. Remove pan from heat, cover, and keep warm in SLOW oven. Place 4 dinner plates in oven to warm.

8 In stockpot, bring 5 ltrs (8 pts) lightly salted water to a boil over high heat.

9 Add noodles to boiling water and cook 3 to 4 minutes for fresh, 8 to 12 minutes for dried. Transfer to colander and drain. Return noodles to pot and toss with 1 tablespoon vegetable oil.

10 Divide noodles among 4 warm dinner plates and top with chicken sausages.

Added touch

Alsatians love their beer almost as much as they love their own wine, and this dark-beer dessert will surprise and delight your palate. It is refreshing, with a taste that is difficult to identify immediately. It is also very easy to make and can be prepared a day or two in avance, if desired.

Dark-Beer Granité

250 g (8 oz) sugar
750 ml (1½ pts) dark beer
1 tablespoon fresh lemon juice

1 In the morning, open beer and allow to flatten.

2 In small heavy-gauge saucepan, combine sugar with 250 ml (8 fl oz) water and bring to a boil over medium heat. Reduce heat and cook, without stirring, 7 to 10 minutes, or until mixture turns a light caramel colour.

3 Remove pan from heat. Add beer very slowly, stirring to combine. Return to heat and stir 2 to 3 minutes, or until smooth.

4 Remove pan from heat and stir in lemon juice. Pour into shallow 22 by 20 cm (9 by 12 inch) pan and allow to cool at least 15 minutes. Place in freezer.

5 After 30 to 40 minutes, 'shave' the beer granité as follows: with a fork, scrape through it several times and return to freezer. After 30 minutes, shave it again. Repeat.

6 Beer granité is ready to serve when totally frozen but in shavings. Divide among balloon wine glasses or small bowls and serve immediately.

<table>
<tr><td>

</td><td>

Marinated Vegetable Salad
Marseillaise Fish Stew with Rouille
and Cheese Croutons

</td></tr>
</table>

This flavourful fish stew is a simple version of *bouillabaisse*, which contains many varieties of fish and shellfish. Here only one type of firm-fleshed fish and mussels are used. The stew is served with *rouille*, a peppery mayonnaise-like sauce.

What to drink
A good wine for this menu would be a dry rosé such as Tavel or a firm, clean Muscadet.

Start-to-Finish Steps
1 Prepare garlic for salad, stew, and rouille.
2 Follow stew recipe steps 1 to 4.
3 Follow salad recipe steps 1 to 6.
4 Follow croutons recipe steps 1 to 3.
5 follow rouille recipe steps 1 to 6.
6 Follow salad recipe step 7.
7 Follow stew recipe steps 5 and 6.
8 Follow croutons recipe step 4 and salad recipe step 8.
9 Follow stew recipe steps 7 to 9 and serve with salad and croutons.

To accentuate the colours and textures of the fish stew, serve it in a large tureen with the rouille *in a separate bowl and a marinated green bean, mushroom and red pepper salad on the side. Keep the cheese croutons warm in a napkin-lined basket.*

Marinated Vegetable Salad

Salt
250 g (¹/₂ lb) green beans
12 to 16 medium-size mushrooms
¹/₂ red bell pepper
1 head lettuce
2 cloves garlic, peeled and crushed
¹/₂ teaspoon freshly ground black pepper
¹/₂ teaspoon Dijon mustard
Juice of 1 lemon
125 ml (4 fl oz) plus 2 tablespoons extra-virgin olive oil

1 In large saucepan bring 2¹/₂ ltrs (4 pts) lightly salted water to a boil over high heat.
2 While water is heating, remove strings and trim stem ends of green beans.
3 Add beans to boiling water and cook 6 to 7 minutes, or until tender but still crisp.

4 While beans are cooking, wipe mushrooms clean with damp paper towels. Cut into 2¹/₂ mm (¹/₈ inch) thick slices. Wash bell pepper and pat dry. Cut into 5 mm (¹/₄ inch) thick strips. Wash lettuce and dry in salad spinner or pat dry with paper towels and refrigerate.
5 Transfer beans to colander, refresh under cold running water, and drain.
6 For vinaigrette, combine garlic, 1 teaspoon salt, pepper, mustard, lemon juice, and oil in medium-size bowl.
7 Fifteen minutes before serving, add beans, mushrooms, and bell pepper to vinaigrette, and toss gently.
8 Divide lettuce among four salad plates and top with marinated vegetables.

Marseillaise Fish Stew

2 leeks
1 fennel bulb (about 500 g (1 lb))
Small bunch parsley
Medium-size onion
2 tablespoons extra-virgin olive oil
3 cloves garlic, peeled and chopped
1 teaspoon dried thyme
1 strip dried orange peel
3 medium-size tomatoes (about 500 g (1 lb) total
    weight)
500 ml (1 pt) dry white wine or vermouth
500 ml (1 pt) fish stock
Pinch of saffron threads
Salt and freshly ground white pepper
750 g (1^1/$_2$ lbs) fillets of firm-fleshed non-oily fish,
    such as bass, snapper, grouper, cod, halibut, etc.
500 g (1 lb) mussels (about 20), cleaned and beards
    removed
Rouille (see following recipe)

1   Trim root ends and upper leaves of leeks, and split
    leeks lengthwise. Gently spread leaves and rinse
    under cold running water. Pat dry with paper
    towels. Cut into 1 cm (^{1}/$_2$ inch) thick semicircles.
    Cut fennel bulb in half and slice into 1 cm (^{1}/$_2$ inch)
    thick pieces. Wash parsley and pat dry. Chop
    enough parsley to measure 30 g (1 oz). Peel and
    chop onion.
2   In large deep non-aluminium skillet, heat olive oil
    over medium heat. Add leeks, fennel, and onion,
    and sauté 1 minute. Add 15 g (^{1}/$_2$ oz) parsley,
    garlic, thyme, and orange peel, and sauté another
    5 minutes, or until tender.
3   Meanwhile, peel, core, seed, and chop tomatoes.
4   Add tomatoes, white wine, stock, saffron, and 500
    ml (1 pt) water, and bring to a boil over high heat.
    Reduce heat to low and simmer, covered, 30
    minutes. Season with salt and white pepper to
    taste.
5   Cut fish into portion-size pieces. Add fish to
    simmering broth and poach 8 to 10 minutes per
    2^1/$_2$ cm (1 inch) thickness.
6   Five minutes before fish should be done, add
    mussels to skillet and cook, covered, 5 minutes, or
    until mussels open. Discard any mussels that do
    not open.
7   Transfer fish and mussels with a slotted spoon to
    a tureen.
8   Taste broth, adjust seasoning, and ladle enough
    broth over fish to barely cover. Garnish with
    chopped parsley.
9   Stir rouille into remaining broth and pour into
    small bowl or sauceboat.

Rouille

125 g (4 oz) jar pimiento
3 cloves garlic, peeled and crushed
1 large fresh basil leaf (optional)
2 eggs
30 g (1 oz) fresh bread crumbs
125 ml (4 fl oz) extra-virgin olive oil
Hot pepper sauce
Salt and freshly ground black pepper

1   Rinse, drain, and chop enough pimiento to measure
    2 level tablespoons
2   Using food processor or a mortar and pestle, purée
    pimiento, garlic, and basil, if using, until paste-like
    but not completely smooth.
3   Separate eggs, adding 1^1/$_2$ yolks to garlic 'paste'
    and reserving whites for another use.
4   Add bread crumbs and process another 5 seconds
    or turn mixture into a small bowl and blend with
    a spoon.
5   With processor running or while stirring, slowly
    drizzle in olive oil, as for mayonnaise, and continue
    to blend until mixture is thick and smooth.
6   Add hot pepper sauce and salt and pepper to taste,
    and stir to blend. Rouille should be very spicy.

Cheese Croutons

3 level tablespoons freshly grated Parmesan cheese
4 level tablespoons unsalted butter, at room
    temperature
1 loaf French bread, preferably day-old
Paprika

1   Preheat oven to 180°C (350°F or Mark 4).
2   In small bowl, blend cheese and butter with fork.
3   Cut bread into 12 slices. Spread one side of each
    slice with cheese-butter mixture and arrange slices
    in a single layer on cookie sheet. Sprinkle tops
    lightly with paprika.
4   Bake 8 to 10 minutes, or until crisp and golden.

<table>
<tr><td>

Menu

3
</td><td>

Braised Artichoke Hearts with Fresh Basil
Coquilles St. Jacques Provençal/Buttered New Potatoes
Mixed Green Salad with Garlic Toast
</td></tr>
</table>

For the braised artichokes, you may prefer to use fresh artichoke bottoms. Buy small artichokes that are not opened or discoloured. To prepare artichokes for cooking, wash them by plunging them in cold water, stems up, then snap off the stems and pull off any tough leaves from around the base. Slice off the top third of each artichoke. Cook artichokes in boiling water for 15 to 45 minutes, depending on size, or until tender, then drain thoroughly. When the artichokes are cool, pull out the centre leaves, scoop out the fuzzy choke with a teaspoon and remove all of the remaining leaves (reserve them to eat at a later time). You are left with artichoke bottoms.

What to drink
Either a white Burgundy, such as a Mâcon or Saint-Véran, or a dry California rosé would be fine here. Muscadet, from the Loire, is also a good choice.

Start-to-Finish Steps
1   Wash lettuce, watercress, radicchio, parsley, and fresh herbs, if using. Dry in salad spinner or pat dry with paper towels. Shred lettuce for artichokes recipe and chop parsley for scallops recipe. Wrap watercress, leaf lettuce, and radicchio in paper towels and refrigerate until ready to assemble salad.
2   Follow artichokes recipe steps 1 to 4.
3   Follow scallop recipe steps 1 to 4 and artichokes recipe step 5.
4   Follow potatoes recipe steps 1 and 2, and scallops recipe steps 5 and 6.
5   Follow salad recipe steps 1 to 3.
6   Follow artichokes recipe steps 6 and 7, and potatoes recipe steps 3 and 4.
7   Follow salad recipe steps 4 and 5.
8   Follow scallops recipe step 7, salad recipe step 6, and serve with artichokes and potatoes.

This elegant meal for family or company features scallops in a tomato sauce, braised artichokes with leeks and fresh basil, and new potatoes. Garnish the mixed green salad of leaf lettuce, watercress, and radicchio with garlic toast triangles.

33

Braised Artichoke Hearts with Fresh Basil

2 leeks
3 level tablespoons unsalted butter
3 tablespoons extra-virgin olive oil
275 g (9 oz) package frozen artichoke hearts
6 cloves garlic, unpeeled
6 large leaves fresh basil, or ½ teaspoon dried
100 g (3 oz) coarsely shredded lettuce
1 bay leaf
Salt and freshly ground pepper
1 to 2 tablespoons chicken stock

1 Trim off root ends of leeks, split lengthwise, and wash thoroughly. Trim off green leaves. Slice white part into 5 mm (¼ inch) semicircles.
2 In heavy-gauge casserole or saucepan, heat 2 tablespoons butter and oil over medium heat. Add leeks, artichoke hearts, and garlic, and cook, covered, 5 minutes, gently separating frozen artichoke hearts and turning to keep them from browning.
3 While vegetables are sweating, slice basil leaves into fine shreds. Reserve 2 sliced basil leaves for garnish.
4 Add basil, lettuce, bay leaf, and salt and pepper to taste to casserole. Cover, reduce heat to low, and cook very gently, stirring occasionally to prevent sticking, 20 to 25 minutes, or until artichokes are tender. If dish becomes too dry during braising, add 1 to 2 tablespoons chicken stock.
5 Place dinner plates under hot running water to warm.
6 Taste mixture and adjust seasoning, if necessary. Remove and discard bay leaf.
7 Remove casserole from heat and swirl in remaining tablespoon of butter to enrich the sauce. Divide among dinner plates and garnish with reserved basil.

Coquilles St. Jacques Provençal

Medium-size onion
4 cloves garlic
750 g (1½ lbs) fresh sea scallops
Salt and freshly ground pepper
4 tablespoons extra-virgin olive oil
4 large tomatoes (about 1¼ kg (2 ½ lbs) total weight)
15 g (½ oz) chopped parsley
1½ tablespoons fresh thyme leaves or
    1½ tablespoons dried
1 bay leaf
250 ml (8 fl oz) dry white wine or 150 ml (5 fl oz) dry vermouth

1 Peel and dice onion. Peel and finely mince garlic.
2 In colander, rinse scallops under cold running water. Pat dry with paper towels. Slice scallops horizontally in half and season with salt and pepper.
3 In large skillet, heat 2 tablespoons olive oil over medium heat. Add scallops and sauté quickly, just until opaque, about 2 minutes. Using slotted spoon, transfer scallops to medium-size bowl.
4 Add remaining olive oil to skillet and return to medium heat. Add onions and garic, and sauté gently about 5 minutes, or until tender.
5 Core, peel, seed, and chop tomatoes.
6 Add tomatoes, parsley, thyme, bay leaf, wine, and accumulated juices from scallops to onion mixture. Cook stirring occasionally, over medium-high heat, about 15 minutes, or until thickened and slightly reduced.
7 Add scallops to tomato mixture and cook just until heated through. Taste and adjust seasoning. Divide among dinner plates.

Buttered New Potatoes

8 small new potatoes (about 625 g (1¼ lbs) total
    weight)
Salt
2 level tablespoons unsalted butter
Freshly ground pepper

1 Scrub potatoes clean, leaving skins on.
2 Place potatoes in medium-size saucepan. Add 1
    teaspoon salt and water to cover, and bring to a
    boil over medium-high heat. Lower heat to medium
    and continue boiling 20 minutes, or until potato
    may be pierced easily with a knife tip.
3 Transfer potatoes to colander and drain.
4 Off heat, add butter to the saucepan and, when
    butter is melted, add potatoes. Tilt and swirl pan
    to coat potatoes evenly. Add salt and pepper to
    taste. Cover and keep warm until ready to serve.

Mixed Green Salad with Garlic Toast

3 level tablespoons unsalted butter
8 slices very thinly sliced white bread
6 large cloves garlic
½ teaspoon salt
Freshly ground pepper
1 teaspoon Dijon mustard
60 ml (2 fl oz) red wine vinegar
125 ml (4 fl oz) extra-virgin olive oil
1 head radicchio
2 bunches watercress
1 head red-leaf lettuce

1 Preheat oven to 170°C (325°F or Mark 3).
2 In small heavy-gauge saucepan or butter warmer,
    melt butter over low heat.
3 Remove crusts from bread and cut each slice on
    the diagonal into two triangles. Brush cookie sheet
    with some of the melted butter and arrange bread
    triangles in a single layer on it. Brush tops of bread
    with remaining melted butter and dry in oven 10
    to 15 minutes. Be careful not to burn bread. The
    toast may be made ahead and stored in an airtight
    container.
4 Remove toast from oven.
5 Peel garlic. In small bowl, mash 2 cloves. Add salt,
    pepper to taste, mustard, vinegar, and oil, and
    whisk until thoroughly blended. Set aside.
6 Place radicchio and greens in large salad bowl.

Pour vinaigrette over salad and toss until evenly
coated. Divide among 4 salad plates. Garnish each
plate with 2 toast triangles and 1 whole garlic clove
for rubbing toast.

Added touch
Herbes de Provence is a mixture of dried herbs, such
as lavender, thyme, rosemary, sage, and basil, that are
frequently used in Provençal cooking and that are
available prepackaged at speciality food shops. If you
prefer, use fresh thyme alone to season this unusual
dessert.

Poached Figs

350 ml (12 fl oz) full-flavoured red wine (Rhône,
    Zinfandel, Rioja)
3 tablespoons honey
½ teaspoon *herbes de Provence*, or 2 sprigs fresh
    thyme
12 fresh figs or 250 g (½ lb) dried figs
60 ml (2 fl oz) heavy cream

1 In medium-size saucepan, bring wine, honey, and
    herbs to a boil over high heat. Reduce heat and
    simmer 5 minutes.
2 Add figs, cover, and simmer gently until tender, 5
    to 10 minutes for fresh, 15 to 20 minutes for dried.
3 With slotted spoon, transfer figs to large bowl.
4 Increase heat to high and reduce poaching liquid
    to a syrupy consistency, about 10 minutes. Pour
    over figs in bowl.
5 Divide figs among individual plates or bowls. Snip
    an 'x' in tops of figs and open them like flowers.
    Pour syrup over them and drizzle heavy cream in
    a thin circle on top of the pool of syrup encircling
    figs. May be served at room temperature or chilled.

Jacques Mokrani

Menu 1
(*Right*)
Shrimp Provençal
Haricots Verts
Salade Macédoine

Restaurateur Jacques Mokrani attributes his culinary talents to his mother. 'I still remember coming home from school at lunchtime famished,' he says. 'On my way up the stairs to our apartment in Algiers, I would be tantalized by the aromas of her fabulous cooking.' Inspired by his mother's meals, he was determined to learn all he could about preparing good food. Today, two classic rules guide his own cooking: in the marketplace, he never settles for second best, purchasing only the freshest seasonal produce and quality meats. And, he always gathers together all food and equipment before starting to cook. He believes that with everything in place a cook can be more creative and efficient.

His menus exemplify the cooking of southern and south-western France. The Provence-inspired main course of Menu 1, shrimp in tomato and garlic sauce, is accompanied by green beans and a *salade macédoine*, which is a variation on the classic mixture of vegetables or fruits. This side dish can be served, French style, as an appetizer.

In Menu 2, the entrée is *tournedos* with sauce *forestière*, which is made with wild mushrooms, Burgundy wine, and heavy cream. A potato *galette* and baked spinach complete the menu.

For Menu 3, Jacques Mokrani presents sautéed chicken pieces and mushrooms in a cream sauce with brandy and sherry. With this, he serves a pilaf and a mixed green salad.

For this colourful Provençal dinner, serve each guest three jumbo shrimp with their tails intact for a more dramatic presentation. Arrange the green beans around the shrimp, or serve them in a separate dish. Curly greens form a base for avocado, tomato, and onion salad.

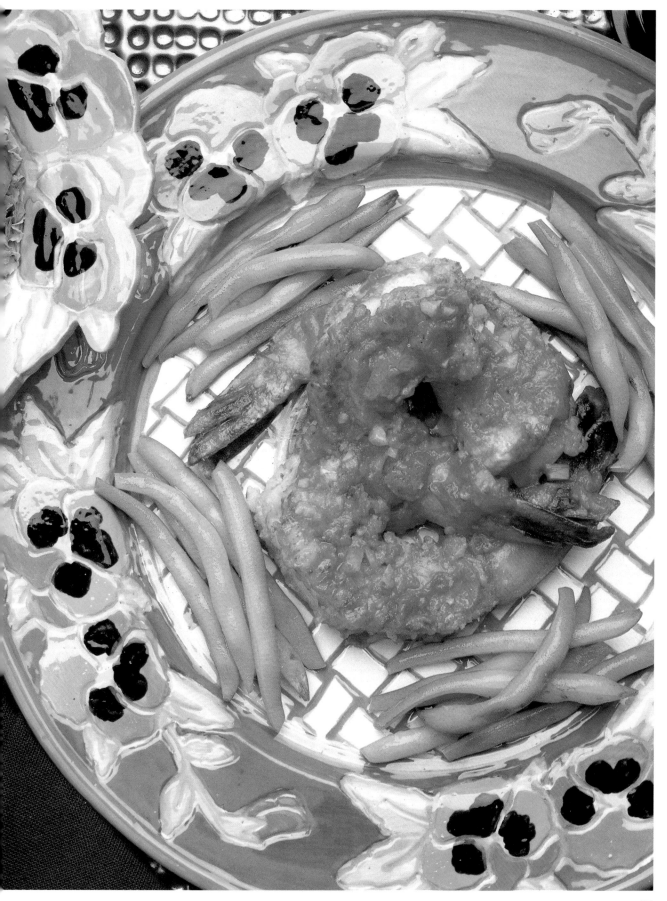

<table>
<tr><td>

Menu

1

</td><td>

Shrimp Provençal
Haricots Verts
Salade Macédoine

</td></tr>
</table>

Dip the jumbo shrimp in milk to tenderize them and then into flour, shaking off any excess. The milk-and-flour coating keeps the shrimp from sticking to the pan and gives them a beautiful golden brown colour.

The sauce Provençal for the shrimp, redolent of garlic is also seasoned with fresh thyme, a herb used frequently in Mediterranean dishes. Fresh thyme is sometimes hard to find in supermarkets or at greengrocers; however, dried thyme is an acceptable substitute.

The string beans are blanched, or plunged quickly into salted boiling water, which brings out their vivid green colour and keeps them from overcooking. Blanching is a classic French technique that preserves the appearance and texture of many vegetables.

For the *salade macédoine*, use ripe avocados that are slightly soft to the touch and have no bruises or dark spots. An unripe avocado will mature quickly left in a paper bag at room temperature for a day or two.

What to drink

A crisp, fruity white wine tastes best with this menu. The first choice is a good California Sauvignon Blanc, but fine alternatives are a French Mâcon or Saint-Véran, or an Italian Sauvignon Blanc or Pinot Grigio.

Start-to-Finish Steps

1 Finely mince garlic for shrimp and sauce recipes.
2 Follow haricots recipe steps 1 to 3.
3 Follow salad reipe steps 1 to 4.
4 Follow haricots recipe steps 4 to 6.
5 Follow shrimp recipe steps 1 to 3.
6 Follow sauce recipe steps 1 to 3.
7 Follow shrimp recipe steps 4 to 9 and serve with haricots and salad.

Shrimp Provençal

12 to 16 jumbo shrimp (about 750 g (1¹/₂ lbs) total weight)
125 ml (4 fl oz) milk
60 g (2 oz) plain flour flour, approximately
1 lemon
125 g (4 oz) unsalted butter
60 ml (2 fl oz) Cognac or other brandy
Small clove garlic, finely minced
Sauce Provençal (see folowing recipe)

1 Peel and devein shrimp, leaving tails intact. Place colander, rinse under cold running water, and drain.
2 Pour milk into pie plate and flour into another pie plate. With tongs, dip shrimp into milk and then into flour to coat thinly; shake off excess. Set aside on waxed paper.
3 Juice lemon and set aside.
4 In large skillet, melt 3 tablespoons butter over medium heat. When butter stops foaming, add shrimp and cook 2 minutes. Turn and cook another 2 minutes, or until golden.
5 While shrimp are cooking, place 4 dinner plates in SLOW oven to warm.
6 Spoon off excess butter from pan. Remove pan from heat and add Cognac or other brandy. Return pan to medium heat and cook, stirring, 1 minute.
7 Add garlic and Sauce Provençale, and stir gently to combine.
8 Add remaining 5 tablespoons butter and lemon juice, and stir until butter is melted and incorporated, about 2 to 3 minutes.
9 Divide shrimp among warm dinner plates and serve immediately.

Sauce Provençal

Two 500g (16 oz) cans Italian plum tomatoes
3 tablespoons olive or vegetable oil
3 medium-size cloves garlic, finely minced
$^1/_2$ teaspoon dried thyme
Bay leaf

1 Drain tomatoes in strainer set over medium-size bowl. Reserve liquid for another use. Chop tomatoes.
2 In large sauté pan, heat oil over medium-high heat until very hot and surface begins to shimmer. Add tomatoes and sauté briefly, about 1 minute.
3 Add garlic, thyme, and bay leaf, and cook, stirring, until tomatoes are reduced and thickened, about 3 minutes. Discard bay leaf. Set sauce aside.

Haricots Verts

Salt
500 g (1 lb) green beans
2 level tablespoons unsalted butter
Freshly ground pepper

1 Preheat oven to SLOW.
2 In large saucepan, bring 2$^1/_2$ ltrs (4 pts) of water and 2 teaspoons salt to a boil over medium-high.
3 Cut off stem ends of beans and remove strings.
4 Add beans to saucepan and let water return to a boil. Blanch 1 to 2 minutes.
5 Transfer beans to colander, refresh under cold running water, and drain. Set aside.
6 In medium-size sauté pan, melt butter over medium heat. Add beans and season with salt and pepper to taste. Sauté, tossing gently, 1 minute. Turn into heatproof bowl and keep warm in oven until ready to serve.

Salade Macédoine

2 medium-size tomatoes
Small red or yellow onion
2 medium-size avocados, preferably the dark, knobby Hass variety
2 tablespoons red wine vinegar
100 ml (3 fl oz) olive oil
Salt and freshly ground pepper
8 leaves escarole or curly endive
Small bunch parsley for garnish (optional)

1 Wash tomatoes and pat dry. Core and cut into wedges. Peel and finely chop enough onion to measure 60 g (2 oz). Peel, pit, and cut avocados into 1$^1/_2$ cm ($^3/_4$ inch) cubes.
2 Combine vegetables in large bowl. Add vinegar, olive oil, and salt and pepper to taste, and toss gently until vegetables are evenly coated with oil.
3 Wash escarole or endive and parsley, if using; pat dry with paper towels. Chop enough parsley to measure 2 tablespoons; set aside.
4 Arrange escarole or endive leaves in individual salad bowls. Top with vegetables and sprinkle with parsley, if desired. Cover and refrigerate until ready to serve.

Added touch
Be sure to allow the caramel to harden completely before adding the crème. As the dessert bakes, the caramel will melt and become a rich sauce. Bake in a soufflé dish placed in a pan of water; this allows the crème to cook slowly and prevents it from either curdling or separating. Covering the crème caramel with foil while baking prevents a 'skin' from forming on the surface.

Crème Caramel

250 g (8 oz) sugar
300 ml (10 fl oz) milk
60 ml (2 fl oz) heavy cream
2 teaspoons vanilla extract
2 whole eggs
1 egg yolk

1 In small saucepan, combine 175 g (6 oz) sugar with 60 ml (2 fl oz) water and cook over high heat, without stirring, until golden brown in colour. Immediately pour caramel into small soufflé dish and let harden completely, preferably overnight.
2 Preheat oven to 170°C (325°F or Mark 3).
3 In medium-size saucepan, bring milk and cream just to boiling point. Immediately set aside to cool until tepid.
4 In medium-size mixing bowl, combine remaining sugar, vanilla, whole eggs, and egg yolk.
5 Add cooled milk and cream to egg mixture and stir until blended.
6 Strain mixture into caramel-coated soufflé dish. Set soufflé dish in a larger pan and add enough water to reach halfway up side of dish. Top dish with a sheet of aluminium foil but do not crimp around edge. Bake 1$^3/_4$ to 2 hours, or until a knife inserted in centre comes out clean.
7 To serve, run a knife around the inside edge of dish to loosen custard. Turn out onto platter, and serve warm or at room temperature.

Menu 2	**Tournedos Forestière** **Potato Galette** **Baked Spinach**

Grated potatoes, seasoned with chopped shallot, nutmeg, and ground pepper, are pressed into a skillet to form the *galette*, or round potato cake. To prevent the potatoes from discolouring, peel and grate them just before cooking. If you must prepare the potatoes ahead of time, put the shreds into a bowl of cold water and then, before cooking, squeeze them dry in paper towels to remove any excess moisture.

Tournedos are small steaks, cut from the eye of the beef tenderloin, close to the tip. These steaks are very tender and require only quick sautéing.

What to drink

Select a good red wine. An appropriate choice here would be a bottle from a Burgundian village such as Nuits-Saint-Georges, Fixin, or Morey-Saint-Denis.

Start-to-Finish Steps

1   Grate whole nutmeg, if using, for potatoes and for spinach. Follow spinach recipe steps 1 to 6.
2   Follow potato recipe steps 1 to 4.
3   While potatoes are cooking, follow sauce recipe steps 1 to 3.
4   Turn potatoes and follow with sauce recipe step 4.
5   Follow spinach recipe step 7 and potato recipe step 5.
6   Follow tournedos recipe steps 1 to 5 and sauce recipe step 5.
7   Follow tournedos recipe step 6 and serve with potatoes and spinach.

Tournedos Forestière

2 tablespoons vegetable oil
Four 135 g to 150 g (4¹/₂ to 5 oz) tournedos (eye of beef tenderloin), 2¹/₂ to 5 cm (1 to 2 inches) thick, trimmed and tied

Good red wine complements the tournedos, *baked spinach, and potato* galette *– an elegant company meal.*

Salt
Small bunch parsley for garnish (optional)
Sauce Forestière (see following recipe)

1 In large skillet, heat oil over high heat until hot but not smoking.
2 While oil is heating, season tournedos on both sides with salt.
3 Place tournedos in skillet and cook each side 3 minutes for rare, 4 to 5 minutes for medium or medium-well, and 6 minutes for well done.
4 While meat is cooking, place dinner plates in SLOW oven to warm.
5 Wash parsley, if using, and pat dry. Finely chop enough parsley to measure 1 level tablespoon.
6 Using metal spatula, transfer tournedos to warm dinner plates and remove string. Top each with a few spoonfuls of Sauce Forestiére and serve garnished with parsley, if desired.

Sauce Forestière

250 g (½ lb) fresh mushrooms
3 level tablespoons unsalted butter
Salt and freshly ground pepper
125 ml (4 fl oz) dry red Burgundy wine
125 ml (4 fl oz) heavy cream

1 Wipe mushrooms clean with damp paper towels. Thinly slice enough mushrooms to measure 250 g (8 oz); set aside.
2 In large skillet, melt butter over medium-high heat. When butter stops foaming, add mushrooms, season with salt and pepper to taste, and sauté, stirring constantly, 4 minutes.
3 Increase heat to high. Add wine and cook, stirring constantly, until liquid is almost evaporated, about 8 minutes.
4 Add heavy cream and cook, stirring, until sauce thickens, about 2 to 3 minutes. Set aside.
5 Reheat sauce over medium heat, stirring occasionally, about 3 minutes.

Potato Galette

Small shallot
750 g (1½ lbs) russet or large new potatoes
Pinch of nutmeg, preferably freshly grated
Salt and freshly ground pepper
5 level tablespoons unsalted butter

1 Peel and finely chop shallot.

2 Fill medium-size bowl two thirds full with cold water. Peel potatoes, dropping each potato into the cold water as you finish peeling it. One by one, pat potatoes dry with paper towels and grate in food processor or with coarse side of grater. Rinse and dry bowl.
3 Comine shallot, potatoes, nutmeg, and salt and pepper to taste in medium-size bowl.
4 In medium-size skillet, melt butter over medium-high heat until sizzling. Add potatoes, pressing them down with back of spoon to make an even round layer. Cover, reduce heat to medium, and cook potatoes 10 minutes. Using 2 large metal spatulas, carefully turn potato cake, pressing down firmly again, and cook potatoes 10 minutes.
5 With 2 spatulas, transfer *galette*, or cake, to large flat ovenproof plate and cut into 8 wedges. Keep warm in oven until ready to serve.

Baked Spinach

Salt
Two 300 g (10 oz) packages frozen chopped spinach
Small onion
2 level tablespoons unsalted butter, approximately
Pinch of nutmeg, preferably freshly grated
Freshly ground pepper
2 eggs
100 ml (3 fl oz) heavy cream

1 Preheat oven to 170°C (325°F or Mark 3). Butter medium-size soufflé dish or baking dish.
2 In medium-size saucepan, bring 500 ml (1 pt) water and 1 teaspoon salt to a boil over medium heat. Add spinach, cover, and simmer 5 minutes.
3 While spinach is simmering, peel and finely chop enough onion to measure 1 tablespoon.
4 Transfer spinach to strainer set over medium-size bowl and press with back of spoon to remove excess moisture. Rinse and dry bowl.
5 In large sauté pan, melt butter over medium-high heat. Add spinach, onion, nutmeg, and salt and pepper to taste. Sauté 3 to 4 minutes, adding more butter if necessary to prevent sticking, or until spinach is heated through. Remove pan from heat.
6 In medium-size bowl, whisk eggs with heavy cream until blended. Add to spinach mixture and stir to combine well. Turn into prepared soufflé dish and bake 25 minutes, or until lightly browned on top.
7 Remove dish from oven, cover loosely with foil, and keep warm on stove top until ready to serve. Reduce oven temperature to SLOW.

Sautéed Chicken Basquaise
Rice Pilaf
Watercress and Belgian Endive Salad

Fresh mushrooms enhance the flavour of the thick wine sauce for this chicken entrée. Shiitake mushrooms, with their velvety brown caps and pronounced aroma fresh are recommended. They are available fresh or dried for Oriental groceries and well-stocked supermarkets. If you cannot find shiitakes, as an alternative, use fresh or dried chanterelles, which are more authentically French. You may find fresh chanterelles (trumpet shaped and golden in colour) at quality greengrocers. Often they are very gritty and should be rinsed quickly under cold running water. Never subject fresh mushrooms to soaking; it destroys their delicate flavour.

What to drink

A medium-bodied dry white wine is called for here. Try a simple French Chablis or Sancerre, or choose a dry California Chenin Blanc or Riesling.

Start-to-Finish Steps

Thirty minutes ahead: If using dried mushrooms, place them in a small bowl with warm water to cover.

1   Follow rice pilaf recipe steps 1 to 4.
2   Follow salad recipes steps 1 to 3.
3   Follow chicken recipe steps 1 to 4.
4   Turn off heat under rice, step 5, and follow chicken recipe steps 5 and 6.

The sautéed chicken in cream sauce flavoured with sherry is accompanied by rice pilaf, mixed salad, and crusty French bread.

5 While sauce is reducing, follow salad recipe steps 4 and 5.
6 Follow chicken recipe step 7 and salad recipe step 6.
7 Follow chicken recipe step 8 and serve with rice and salad.

Sautéed Chicken Basquaise

4 level tablespoons unsalted butter
1 frying chicken, cut into 8 pieces, or 8 chicken thighs (about 1 Kg (2 lb) total weight)
Salt
Freshly ground black pepper
2 medium-size shallots
250 g (1/2 lb) fresh shiitake or chanterelle mushrooms, or 125 g (4 oz) dried chanterelles, reconstituted
1 red bell pepper for garnish (optional)
Small bunch parsley for garnish (optional)
60 ml (2 fl oz) brandy or Cognac
125 ml (4 fl oz) dry sherry
150 ml (5 fl oz) heavy cream

1 In large skillet, melt butter over medium-high heat.
2 While butter is melting, season chicken pieces with salt and pepper to taste.
3 Add chicken pieces to skillet and cook on one side 4 to 5 minutes, or until brown. Using tongs, turn chicken and cook another 4 to 5 minutes.
4 While chicken is browning, peel and chop enough shallots to measure 3 level tablespoons. If using fresh mushrooms, rinse under cold water, pat dry with paper towels, and cut in half. If using reconstituted dried mushrooms, rinse under cold running water and pat dry with paper towels; cut in half. If using red bell pepper or parsley for garnish, wash and pat dry. Core, halve, and seed pepper. Cut into 2 1/2 mm (1/8 inch) wide strips. Trim parsley and chop enough to measure 1 tablespoon. Set aside
5 When chicken has browned, spoon off fat. Remove skillet from heat and add brandy or Cognac. Return skillet to low heat and, using wooden spoon, scrape up any brown bits clinging to pan, stirring to combine with liquid. Continue cooking until brandy is almost evaporated.
6 Add shallots and mushrooms to skillet, and stir gently to combine. Add sherry and continue cooking over low heat, stirring, until liquid is reduced by half, about 7 minutes.
7 Stir in cream and simmer until sauce is thick enough to coat a wooden spoon, about 5 minutes.
8 Divide chicken pieces among dinner plates. Top with mushroom sauce, and serve garnished with parsley or topped with red pepper strips, if desired.

Rice Pilaf

Small bunch scallions
2 level tablespoons unsalted butter
625 ml (1 1/4 pts) chicken stock, preferably homemade
2 to 3 whole cloves
175 g (6 oz) converted long-grain rice

1 Chop enough scallions to measure 2 level tablespoons.
2 In medium-size heavy-gauge saucepan, melt butter over low heat. Add scallions and sauté until wilted, about 2 minutes.
3 Add stock and 2 to 3 cloves, according to taste, increase heat to high, and bring to a rolling boil.
4 Stir in rice and return mixture to a boil. Cover, reduce heat to very low, and simmer until the rice has absorbed all the stock, about 18 minutes.
5 Turn off heat and cover until ready to serve.

Watercress and Belgian Endive Salad

1 lemon
2 bunches watercress
2 small heads Belgian endive
1 egg
1/2 teaspoon sugar
1/4 teaspoon salt
Freshly ground white pepper
1 teaspoon white wine vinegar
125 ml (4 fl oz) olive oil

1 Squeeze lemon to measure 2 tablespoons juice.
2 Immerse watercress in large bowl of cold water and agitate to disolve any grit. Trim off stems and discard. Drain watercress in colander and dry in salad spinner or pat dry with paper towels. Place in large salad bowl.
3 Wash endive and slice into 1 cm (1/2 inch) thick rounds; add to watercress in salad bowl. Cover bowl with plastic wrap and refrigerate until ready to serve.
4 Using two small bowls, separate egg white and yolk, reserving white for another use. Add lemon juice, salt, and pepper to taste, and whisk until salt is dissolved. Add vinegar and whisk briskly until bubbles appear on surface.
5 In a slow, steady stream, add olive oil to mixture, whisking continuously until dressing acquires a creamy texture. Refrigerate until ready to serve.
6 Just before serving, pour dressing over salad and toss gently. Divide among individual plates.

John Case

Menu 1
(*Left*)
Tomato and Celery Root Salad
with Chèvre Dressing
Black Bass with Fennel and Romaine
Saffron Rice

French regional recipes, with their emphasis on fresh indigenous produce, suit John Case's style of cooking: 'I try to preserve the character and integrity of each ingredient, and I use local seasonal foods when I cook,' he says. For him, this means no elaborate sauces or multiplicity of ingredients.

For his three menus, he selects dishes representative of Provence, Lyons, and Périgord, respectively. The black bass main dish of Menu 1 is reminiscent of a Provençal speciality, sea bass grilled with fennel stalks are covered with Romaine leaves and baked. Saffron colours and flavours the accompanying rice.

Menu 2 highlights foods that are associated with the city of Lyons: poultry, here prepared as stuffed chicken breasts, and potatoes, which the cook shreds and forms into a pie. John Case's third menu features omelettes filled with mushrooms, a Périgourdine speciality. The stuffed vegetables contain a variety of herbs, cheeses, and nuts.

Black bass fillets, flavoured with sliced fennel, are covered with Romaine leaves to make an appetizing entrée for an informal dinner. Golden saffron rice accompanies the fish. For the salad, arrange tomato slices and coarsely grated celery root decoratively on side plates, and garnish with a stem of arugula.

Tomato and Celery Root Salad with Chèvre Dressing
Black Bass with Fennel and Romaine
Saffron Rice

Crisp slices of fennel bake with the black bass and impart a slight anise flavour. Florence fennel, or *finocchio*, has a flattened bulbous base and long green stalks. Select firm bulbs without brown spots. Fennel is usually available from September to April, with December being its peak month. If you cannot find it, use the same amount of sliced celery plus $1/2$ teaspoon fennel seed, or aniseed, for a similar flavour.

What to drink

A crisp dry white wine would counter the richness of this menu. Try a California Sauvignon Blanc, a Pouilly-Fumé, or a white Bordeaux, such as Entre-Deux-Mers.

Start-to-Finish Steps

1 Follow rice recipe steps 1 and 2.
2 While onion is wilting, follow bass recipe step 1.
3 Follow rice recipe steps 3 to 5.
4 Follow bass recipe steps 2 to 5.
5 Follow salad recipe steps 1 and 2, and rice recipe step 6.
6 Follow bass recipe step 6 and salad recipe steps 3 and 4.
7 Follow bass recipe step 7, rice recipe step 7, and serve with salad.

Tomato and Celery Root Salad with Chèvre Dressing

Large clove garlic
Small bunch arugula or watercress
2 to 3 large leaves fresh basil, or 1 teaspoon dried
125 g ($1/4$ lb) mild chèvre, preferably Montrachet, or feta cheese
60 ml (2 fl oz) balsamic, red wine, or tarragon vinegar
175 ml (6 fl oz) olive oil or light vegetable oil
4 medium-size tomatoes (about 625 g ($1 1/4$ lbs))
Large celery root (about 350 g ($3/4$ lb) total weight)

1 Peel garlic and cut in half. Wash arugula or watercress and fresh basil, if using, and pat dry with paper towels. Trim off stem ends. Cut chèvre into small chunks.
2 In food processor or blender, combine garlic,

basil, chèvre, vinegar, and oil, and purée until smooth, about 1 minute. Leave dressing in processor.
3 Wash, core, and cut each tomato crosswise into 4 slices. Peel celery root and grate coarsely, or cut into $2 1/2$ mm ($1/8$ inch) julienne strips. Divide tomato slices equally among 4 salad plates. Mound celery root beside tomatoes and garnish each serving with a stem of arugula.
4 Just before serving, process dresing to recombine and spoon over each salad.

Black Bass with Fennel and Romaine

Large fennel bulb (about 500g (1 lb)
Four 175 to 250 g (6 to 8 oz) black bass fillets, each about 1 cm ($1/2$ inch) thick
2 medium-size cloves garlic
75 ml ($2 1/2$ fl oz) dry white wine
125 g (4 oz) unsalted butter
6 to 8 leaves Romaine

1 Preheat oven to 180°C (350°F or Mark 4). Cut off bulbous base of fennel. Separate stalks, wash in cold water, and pat dry. Select 8 to 10 stalks and reserve remainder for another use (see *Leftover suggestion*). Cut each stalk in half crosswise. Peel and mince garlic.
2 In large skillet, bring 1 cm ($1/2$ inch) of water to a boil. Add fennel, cover, and simmer until crisp-tender, about 10 minutes.
3 While fennel is simmering, melt 4 level tablespoons butter in small saucepan over low heat.
4 Rinse bass fillets under cold running water and pat dry with paper towels. Generously grease shallow baking dish. Place fish in dish and sprinkle each fillet with one quarter of the minced garlic. Pour wine over fish and dot each fillet with butter, cut into small pieces, and top with 4 slices of fennel. Brush with half of melted butter.
5 Bake fish 10 to 15 minutes, depending on thickness of fillets, just until firm but undercooked.
6 Wash Romaine leaves and dry in salad spinner or pat dry with paper towels. Drape Romaine leaves loosely over fish, and brush with remaining melted

butter. Bake another 5 minutes, or until fish is still firm but flaky.

7 Divide fillets among dinner plates.

Saffron Rice

Small onion
1 level tablespoon unsalted butter
1 teaspoon saffron threads (about 15 g ($^1/_2$ oz))
175 g (6 oz) long-grain white rice
625 ml (1$^1/_4$ pts) chicken stock, preferably homemade
1 teaspoon salt

1 Peel and chop enough onion to measure about 60 g (2 oz).
2 In medium-size saucepan, melt butter over medium heat. Add onion and sauté 3 to 5 minutes, or until soft and translucent.
3 Stir in saffron threads and sauté about 1 minute.
4 Add rice and cook, stirring, about 3 minutes, or until rice is evenly coloured, heated through, and translucent.
5 While rice is cooking, bring chicken stock to a boil in small saucepan over high heat. Pour stock over rice, add salt, and cover. Reduce heat to low and simmer rice gently 15 to 20 minutes, or until stock is just absorbed.
6 Turn off heat and allow rice to stand, covered, until ready to serve.
7 Fluff rice with fork and divide among dinner plates.

Added touch
Instead of a raspberry-cream filling for this delicate, airy cake, you can use any kind of berries in season, diced peaches, or sliced bananas.

Walnut Meringue Torte

125 g (4 oz) walnuts
6 large eggs
$^1/_2$ teaspoon salt
400 g (14 oz) plus 4 teaspoons sugar
$^1/_2$ teaspoon vanilla extract
60 ml (2 fl oz) apple cider vinegar
350 ml (12 fl oz) heavy cream
250 g (8 oz) raspberries, washed and hulled
Confectioners' sugar for garnish

1 Preheat oven to 180°C (350°F or Mark 4).
2 Arrange walnuts in a single layer in baking pan. Toast in oven, shaking pan occasionally to prevent scorching, 12 minutes or until golden brown. Remove from oven and allow to cool. Raise oven temperature to 190°C (375°F or Mark 5).
3 For meringue, separate eggs, reserving yolks for another use. Combine egg whites and salt in medium-size bowl. Using electric mixer, beat until foamy. While still beating, gradually add 350 g (12 oz) sugar and beat until stiff peaks form.
4 In food processor or with nut grinder, grind walnuts. Add nuts, vanilla, and vinegar to egg whites, and beat with electric mixer on slow speed until blended.
5 Butter two 20 cm (8 inch) round cake pans and then line with buttered waxed paper. Sprinkle with flour and tilt pans to coat evenly.
6 Divide batter between pans and bake 30 to 40 minutes, or until meringue pulls away from sides of pans. Wash mixing bowl and beaters, dry, and put in refrigerator to chill.
7 Cool meringues in pans for 10 minutes and turn out onto rack. Remove waxed paper and cool completely.
8 In chilled bowl, whip heavy cream with chilled beaters until stiff peaks form.
9 For torte base, spread one meringue with two thirds of the whipped cream and sprinkle with remaining sugar. Reserving 8 raspberries for top, spread raspberies over cream.
10 Top filling with second meringue. Spread half of remaining whipped cream over top meringue layer.
11 Fit pastry bag with star tip, fill with remaining whipped cream, and pipe 8 rosettes on top layer. Place a raspberry in each rosette, and lightly dust entire top of torte with confectioners' sugar.

Leftover suggestion
Mince extra fennel leaves finely and use them as a garnish for soups, salads, and vegetable dishes. Trim any remaining fennel stalks to serve with cheese dips, or slice them into a tossed salad.

<table>
<tr><td></td><td>

Lettuce Salad with Orange-Lemon Dressing
Ballotines of Chicken
Shredded Potato Pie
</td></tr>
</table>

For an impressive buffet, serve rolled and stuffed chicken breasts with shredded potatoes that have been baked in an attractive pie dish – or unmould the potatoes if you prefer. Offer the salad on a decorative platter.

Ballotine is a French culinary term describing boned meat, fowl, or fish that is stuffed, rolled, and then skewered into a 'bundle' shape for cooking. Here, John Case uses boneless chicken breasts with the skins on and makes a filling of chicken livers, mushrooms, and onions.

What to drink
For this menu, the cook suggests a white Burgundy, such as a Mâcon. You could also try a Beaujolais.

Start-to-Finish Steps
1 Follow potato recipe steps 1 to 3.
2 Follow chicken recipe steps 1 to 5.
3 Follow salad recipe steps 1 to 4.
4 Follow chicken recipe step 6 and salad recipe step 5.
5 Follow chicken recipe step 7 and serve with salad and potato pie.

Lettuce Salad with Orange-Lemon Dressing

2 heads Bibb lettuce
Medium-size red onion
2 small cloves garlic
3 oranges
1 lemon
1 egg
1 tablespoon Dijon mustard
1 tablespoon red wine vinegar
100 ml (3 fl oz) olive oil
Salt and freshly ground black pepper

1 Wash lettuce leaves and dry in salad spinner or pat dry with paper towels. Peel onion. In food processor fitted with slicing disc or with chef's knife, cut onion into paper-thin slices. Peel and chop garlic.
2 Arrange lettuce leaves on platter, or on 4 individual plates, if preferred, and top with half of the onion rings.
3 With paring knife, peel 2 oranges, removing as much white pith as possible. Segment oranges by cutting along both sides of membranes, or cut

crosswise into 5 mm (¹/₄ inch) thick slices. Arrange oranges over onion and lettuce and top with remaining onion rings. Cover and refrigerate until ready to serve.

4   Juice remaining orange and lemon. In small bowl, combine the fruit juices, egg, and mustard. Add garlic and remaining ingredients, and whisk until blended.

5   Just before serving, whisk dressing to recombine and spoon over salad.

Ballotines of Chicken

250 g (¹/₂ lb) chicken livers
250 g (¹/₂ lb) mushrooms
4 level tablespoons unsalted butter
Small yellow onion, peeled and chopped
4 sprigs parsley, chopped
1 teaspoon ground allspice
4 boneless chicken breasts, with skin attached (each about 250 g (¹/₂ lb))
Salt and freshly ground black pepper
1 level tablespoon flour
125 ml (4 fl oz) dry red wine, or white wine, if preferred

1   Preheat oven to 230°C (450°F or Mark 8). Rinse chicken livers, pat dry with paper towels, and remove membranes and fat. Wipe mushrooms clean with damp paper towels and chop.

2   In medium-size skillet, melt 2 level tablespoons butter over medium heat. Add chicken livers, mushrooms, onion, parsley, and allspice, and sauté, stirring continuously, 5 to 7 minutes, or until livers are no longer pink.

3   Transfer sautéed chicken livers to food processor or blender and purée until smooth; set aside.

4   Place each chicken breast between 2 sheets of waxed paper and pound with mallet or rolling pin to 5 mm (¹/₄ inch) thickness. Place each breast skin side down and season with salt and pepper. Mound one fourth of liver mixture in centre of each breast. Fold sides of breast over filling and secure with toothpicks or small skewers.

5   Place ballotines in medium-size roasting pan skin side up and dot each with about ¹/₂ tablespoon butter. Bake until skin is brown, juices run clear, and meat is tender when pierced with a skewer, 20 to 25 minutes.

6   Transfer ballotines to serving platter, remove toothpicks, and cover loosely with foil to keep warm.

7   Pour off all but 1 tablespoon fat from roasting pan. Stir in flour and cook over medium heat, stirring,

1 minute. Add red or white wine to deglaze pan, scraping up any bits of chicken from bottom of pan. Strain sauce through sieve set over small bowl. Pour sauce over chicken and serve.

Shredded Potato Pie

Large yellow onion
3 large potatoes (about 750 g (1¹/₂ lbs) total weight)
3 level tablespoons unsalted butter
250 ml (8 fl oz) milk
3 eggs, lightly beaten
60 g (2 oz) freshly grated Parmesan cheese
Salt and freshly ground white pepper

1   Peel onion and potatoes. In food processor fitted with shredding disc or with coarse side of grater, shred onion and potatoes. In colander, rinse shredded vegetables under cold water, drain well, pressing with back of spoon to remove water, and pat dry with paper towels.

2   In medium-size saucepan, combine butter and milk, and heat over medium heat just until butter melts. Stir in shredded potato-onion mixture, eggs, Parmesan, and salt and pepper to taste, and cook, tossing until mixture is combined and heated through.

3   Generously butter a 22 cm (9 inch) ovenproof pie dish. Turn mixture into dish, and bake, uncovered, in 230°C (450°F or Mark 8) oven 45 minutes, or until crisp and lightly browned.

<table>
<tr><td>

Menu

3

</td><td>

Wild Mushroom Omelettes
Stuffed Vegetables

</td></tr>
</table>

For a family supper or Sunday brunch, offer each guest a mushroom-filled omelette and a selection of stuffed vegetables.

Before you make the omelettes, have the rest of the menu prepared and your guests seated. You will be able to cook and serve four omelettes in less than fifteen minutes. For a puffier omelette, bring the eggs to room temperature. Use a non-stick or well-seasoned pan to keep the eggs from sticking, and make sure it is hot before you add the butter and the eggs. It is the right temperature when a drop of water skitters on the surface.

What to drink

For a festive touch, the cook suggests you serve a sparkling wine. Choose one from Touraine or the Loire Valley, or try a California Brut.

Start-to-Finish Steps

One hour ahead: Set out eggs for omelettes. For vegetables recipe, set out cream cheese.

Ten minutes ahead: Clarify butter for omelettes.

1 Follow vegetables recipe steps 1 to 9.
2 Follow omelettes recipe steps 1 to 9, vegetables recipe 10, and serve.

Wild Mushroom Omelettes

250 g (¹/₂ lb) shiitakes, chanterelles, crèpes, oyster, or
  other fresh mushrooms
Large shallot
6 level tablespoons unsalted butter, clarified
2 tablespoons dry white vermouth
12 large eggs
Salt and freshly ground white pepper
1 teaspoon Worcestershire sauce

1 Wipe mushrooms clean with damp paper towels.
   Trim off stems, reserving for another use, and cut
   mushrooms into 2¹/₂ mm (¹/₈ inch) thick slices.
   Peel and mince shallot; set aside.
2 Place 4 dinner plates under hot running water to
   warm.
3 In medium-size skillet, heat 2 tablespoons clarified
   butter over medium heat. Add shallots and sauté
   2 to 3 minutes, or until soft. Add three quarters of
   sliced mushrooms and sauté 3 to 5 minutes, or just
   until tender. Stir in dry vermouth. Remove from
   heat and cover to keep warm.
4 Whisk eggs with salt and white pepper to taste.
   Add Worcestershire and whisk until foamy.
5 Dry dinner plates.
6 Add 2 teaspoons clarified butter to omelette pan,
   tilting pan so that sides are evenly coated, and
   place pan over medium heat. When pan is hot,
   add one quarter of egg mixture and allow to set,
   about ¹/₂ minute. With fork, gently pull cooked
   edges toward centre of pan, tilting pan so uncooked
   egg runs to edges, about 3 minutes.
7 Place one quarter of sautéed mushrooms on
   portion of omelette near handle of pan. Tilt pan
   and, using fork, fold omelette over mushrooms
   toward handle. Then roll folded, filled omelette
   onto warm plate.
8 Repeat steps 6 and 7 three more times.
9 Garnish omelettes with remaining sliced
   mushrooms.

Stuffed Vegetables

2 baby aubergines
4 medium-size tomatoes (about 350 g (³/₄ lb) total
  weight)
8 to 12 extra-large mushrooms with 5 cm (2 inch)
  wide caps
1 clove garlic
45 g (1¹/₂ oz) fresh bread crumbs
Salt and freshly ground black pepper
1 or 2 fresh basil leaves, or ¹/₂ teaspoon dried
3 tablespoons vegetable oil
60 g (2 oz) cream cheese, at room temperature
30 g (1 oz) freshly grated Parmesan cheese
1 level tablespoon pine nuts
1 level tablespoon capers, drained

1 Wash aubergines and tomatoes, and pat dry. Cut
   aubergines in half lengthwise and scoop out pulp,
   leaving 5 mm (¹/₄ inch) shell. Reserve pulp. Cut 5
   mm (¹/₄ inch) thick slice from tops of tomatoes
   and scoop out pulp. Reserve pulp. Wipe
   mushrooms clean with damp paper towels. Trim
   off stems. Dice stems, tops, and reserved pulp.
   Peel and mince garlic.
2 In medium-size bowl, combine diced vegetable
   mixture, garlic, bread crumbs, and salt and pepper
   to taste.
3 For tomatoes, wash fresh basil, if using, pat dry,
   and chop.
4 Preheat oven to 200°C (400°F or Mark 6).
5 In small skillet, heat 1 tablespoon oil over medium
   heat. Add one third of vegetable mixture and
   sauté 2 minutes.
6 For stuffing aubergines: Add cream cheese to
   sautéed vegetable mixture and stir until combined
   and heated through. Divide stuffing between
   aubergines. Wipe out pan with paper towels.
7 For stuffing tomatoes: Add 1 tablespoon oil to pan
   and return to medium heat. Add one third of
   vegetable mixture and sauté 2 minutes. Add basil
   and Parmesan, and stir until combined and heated
   through. Divide stuffing among tomatoes. Wipe
   out pan with paper towels.
8 Add 1 tablespoon oil to pan and return to medium
   heat. Add remainder of vegetable mixture and
   sauté 2 minutes. Add ¹/₂ tablespoon pine nuts and
   capers, and sauté 1 minute. Divide stuffing among
   mushrooms.
9 Place the stuffed vegetables in large shallow
   baking dish. Bake 15 to 20 minutes, or until
   stuffing is browned and vegetables are cooked.
10 Cut aubergines in half crosswise. Divide vegetables
   among dinner plates and garnish mushrooms
   with remaining pine nuts.

Dennis Gilbert

Menu 1
(*Right*)
Tourte à la Périgourdine
Mixed Green Salad

Dennis Gilbert describes himself as a man who cooks for the love of it, acknowledging that his travels through northern Europe have been a major influence upon his food career, as were his experiences as a student and amateur cook at the University of Iowa. He has worked as a professional cook in a number of restaurants, and now is head chef at a restaurant in Maine. He believes that the presentation of a meal is very important, but that dining is more than looking and smelling. 'People should have a substantial meal to sit down to.'

For that reason, he has selected three menus from Périgord and the Auvergne, where sizable meals are commonplace. Menu 1 features *tourte à la périgourdine*, an adaptation of chicken pie that is ideal for a winter supper. *Tourte* comes from the Latin *tortus*, which means making round.

Menu 2, from the Auvergne, offers sautéed chicken breasts and *aligot*, a potato and cheese casserole. The word comes from *aligoter*, 'to cut,' and in a true *aligot* the melted cheese forms long ribbons that have to be cut when the dish is served.

Menu 3, also Auvergnac, consisits of sautéed veal scallops with three distinctive side dishes: saffron apples, lentils with tomatoes and bacon, and a salad of celery root and sorrel. The lentil dish, according to Dennis Gilbert, originated in the town of Le Puy.

The golden crust of the main-dish chicken pie is flecked with chopped parsley and decorated with pastry leaves. Garnish the mixed green salad with grated Parmesan and, if you wish, serve warm French bread as an accompaniment.

Tourte à la Périgourdine
Mixed Green Salad

For his version of this poultry pie, the cook uses fresh mushrooms and chicken livers in place of the truffles and *foie gras* of the traditional Périgord dish. Select chicken livers that are plump, moist, odour free, and dark red. Trim away any membrane and fat before cooking. Madeira, a fortified wine with a sediment, should be recorked after opening and stored on its side.

What to drink

A medium-bodied red wine would best accompany this hearty menu. Good choices include a Saint-Émilion or a California Zinfandel or Merlot.

Start-to-Finish Steps

Thirty minutes ahead: For tourte recipe, chill 750 g (2¹/₂ oz) butter and 75 g (2¹/₂ oz) lard in freezer; clarify 125 g (4 oz) plus 1 level tablespoon butter and set aside.

1 Follow tourte recipe steps 1 to 9.
2 Follow salad recipe step 1.
3 Follow tourte recipe step 10.
4 While tourte is baking, follow salad recipe steps 2 and 3.
5 Follow tourte recipe step 11 and salad recipe step 4.
6 Follow tourte recipe step 12 and serve with salad.

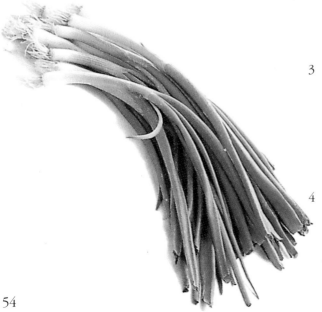

Tourte à la Périgourdine

Pastry:
1 bunch parsley
300 g (10 oz) cups plain flour, approximately
1 teaspoon salt
75 g (21/2 oz) butter, well chilled
75 g (21/2 oz), lard chilled

Filling:
500 g (1 lb) skinless, boneless chicken breasts
250 g (¹/₂ lb) chicken livers
250 g (¹/₂ lb) mushrooms
2 to 3 large shallots
2 cloves garlic
Medium-size tomato
125 g (4 oz) plus 1 level tablespoon unsalted butter, clarified
3 level tablespoons plain flour
350 ml (12 fl oz) cups chicken stock
175 ml (6 fl oz) Madeira wine
³/₄ teaspoon dried marjoram
³/₄ teaspoon fennel seed
Salt and freshly ground black pepper
1 egg

1 Wash parsley and pat dry with paper towels. Chop enough to measure 30 g (1 oz); set aside.
2 In large mixing bowl, combine 250 g (8 oz) flour and salt. Using pastry cutter, or two knives, cut in chilled butter and lard until mixture resembles coarse cornmeal. Stir in parsley. Sprinkle dough with about 60 ml (2 fl oz) iced water, and mix gently with fork to form ball.
3 Grease 22 cm (9 inch) pie plate. On lightly floured surface, roll out two thirds of pastry into a circle large enough to line pie plate. Roll pastry loosely around pin and unroll over pie plate, gently fitting the pastry into the plate. Roughly trim edges and set in freezer to chill thoroughly. Roll out remaining dough to form top crust. Place between 2 sheets of waxed paper and refrigerate.
4 Cut chicken breasts into 1 cm (¹/₂ inch) cubes. Wash chicken livers and pat dry with paper towels. Remove membranes and trim off any excess fat. Wipe mushrooms clean with damp paper towels and cut into 5 mm (¹/₄ inch) thick slices. Peel and mince shallots and garlic. Wash tomato and pat dry.

Peel, core, halve, seed, and chop tomato. Set prepared ingredients aside.

5 Preheat oven to 230°C (450°F or Mark 8). In large skillet, heat 60 g (2 fl oz) clarified butter over medium-high heat. Add chicken cubes, livers, and mushrooms, and sauté, stirring constantly, 5 minutes. With slotted spoon, transfer mixture to large bowl.

6 For sauce, add remaining clarified butter to skillet. Still over medium-high heat, add shallots and garlic, and sauté, stirring constantly, 3 minutes. Sprinkle with 3 level tablespoons flour and cook, stirring, about 2 minutes, or until light brown.

7 Slowly add 350 ml (12 fl oz) stock, whisking constantly to prevent lumps. When sauce is smooth, stir in Madeira, chopped tomato, marjoram, fennel seed, and salt and pepper to taste, and bring to a boil, stirring constantly.

8 Add enough sauce (about $^1/_2$ cup) to chicken mixture to moisten well; reserve remaining sauce.

9 Turn chicken mixture into chilled shell. Cover with top crust, crimping edges of pastry together to seal. Cut 5 or 6 small leaf shapes from pastry trimmings and arrange decoratively in centre of pie. Bake tourte 10 minutes.

10 In small bowl, beat egg with a fork. Remove tourte from oven and reduce temperature to 180°C (350°F or Mark 4). Brush top of crust with beaten egg to glaze and bake another 15 minutes, or until top is golden.

11 Just before serving, return reserved sauce to medium heat for 5 minutes, or until heated through. Pour sauce through strainer set over small pitcher or sauceboat.

12 Remove tourte from oven and serve with sauce.

Mixed Green Salad

Large head Bibb lettuce
Large head red leaf lettuce
1 lemon
 60 ml (2 fl oz) plus 2 tablespoons extra-virgin olive oil
60 g (2 oz) Parmesan cheese
Salt and freshly ground black pepper

1 Wash lettuce and dry in salad spinner or pat dry with paper towels. Tear greens into bite-size pieces, place in salad bowl, cover with plastic wrap, and refrigerate until ready to serve.

2 Squeeze enough lemon to measure about 2 tablespoons juice. In small bowl, combine olive oil and lemon juice and beat vigorously with fork until blended; set aside.

3 Grate enough Parmesan to measure 60 g (2 oz); set aside.

4 Just before serving, beat dressing to recombine and pour over salad greens. Toss greens until evenly coated, season with salt and pepper to taste, and sprinkle generously with grated Parmesan.

Added touch

This cake has a very moist, almost pudding-like texture. Use canned, unsweetened chestnut purée to save time or, if preferred, use canned peeled chestnuts.

Chestnut Cake

450 g ($15^1/_2$ oz) can unsweetened chestnut purée
250 ml (8 fl oz) heavy cream, plus 250 ml (8 fl oz) (optional)
100 g (3 fl oz) walnut-flavoured liqueur (Nociello or eau-de-noix)
250 g (8 oz) butter, at room temperature
350 g (12 oz) sugar
8 eggs, separated
$^1/_4$ teaspoon cream of tartar
1 tablespoon maple syrup (optional)

1 Preheat oven to 190°C (375°F or Mark 5).

2 Butter and flour 25 cm (10 inch) springform pan. In medium-size saucepan, combine chestnut purée, 250 ml (8 fl oz) heavy cream, and liqueur, and bring to a simmer over medium heat. Set aside and allow to cool to room temperature.

3 In bowl of electric mixture, cream butter and 250 ml (8 fl oz) sugar. One at a time, add egg yolks to butter-sugar mixture, beating after each addition until thoroughly blended.

4 In another bowl, beat egg whites and cream of tartar until frothy. Still beating, slowly add remaining sugar and continue to beat until whites are stiff but not dry.

5 With electric mixer at lowest setting, add chestnut purée to creamed butter-egg mixture and beat just until blended.

6 With a rubber spatula, fold egg whites quickly into chestnut batter. Turn mixture into springform pan, smooth top, and bake 1 hour and 20 minutes, or until cake is set but still slightly underdone in centre. Allow to cool to room temperature before unmoulding.

7 Just before serving, whip heavy cream and maple syrup with chilled beaters in chilled bowl until stiff. Unmould cake and serve garnished with maple-flavoured whipped cream, if desired.

Sautéed Chicken Breasts with Vegetables and Summer Savory Butter
Aligot

Carrots and parsnips, are usually available year round in supermarkets. Summer savory, has a robust, peppery taste, somewhat like that of thyme. Either fresh or dried savory will do for this recipe, and herb butter can be made ahead and stored for 2 or 3 weeks in the refrigerator. Incorporating a herb butter into a reduced stock, as in this recipe, makes the sauce shimmer and produces a very flavourful result. For the potato casserole, or *aligot*, use a strong Cheddar cheese.

What to drink
An ideal wine for this dinner is a Gewürztraminer – a dry and spicy one from Alsace or a fruitier California. Either will enrich the sauce for the chicken breasts.

Start-to-Finish Steps
One hour ahead: For summer savory butter, set out 175 g (6 oz) butter to bring to room temperature.

Fifteen minutes ahead: Clarify 3 level tablespoons of butter for chicken recipe.

1 For savory butter and aligot, wash parsley and summer savory; pat dry. Chop enough parsley to measure 4 tbsps and enough savory to measure 1 tbsp. Peel and mince garlic and shallots.
2 Follow savory butter recipe step 1.
3 Follow aligot recipe steps 1 and 2.
4 Follow chicken recipe step 1.
5 Follow aligot recipe steps 3 to 5.
6 Follow chicken recipe steps 2 and 3.
7 While vegetables are cooking, follow savory butter recipe steps 2 to 4.
8 Follow chicken recipe steps 4 to 9 and aligot recipe step 6.
9 Follow chicken recipe step 10 and serve with aligot.

White china emphazises the colours and textures of this elegant meal: chicken with vegetables and potato aligot.

Sautéed Chicken Breasts with Vegetables and Summer Savory Butter

4 skinless, boneless chicken breasts (about 1^1/$_2$ kg (3 lbs) total weight)
250 g (^{1}/$_2$ lb) parsnips
250 g (^{1}/$_2$ lb) carrots
3 level tablespoons unsalted butter plus 3 level tablespoons, clarified
Freshly ground black pepper
2 tablespoons chopped fresh parsley
125 ml (4 fl oz) dry white wine
250 g (8 fl oz) chicken stock, preferably homemade
175 g (6 oz) Summer Savory Butter (see following recipe)

1 Trim chicken breasts. With meat pounder or rolling pin, gently flatten breasts to about 1 cm (^{1}/$_2$ inch) thickness. Split breasts in half, and pat dry on paper towels. Set aside.
2 Peel parsnips and halve lengthwise. Lay flat sides down and cut on diagonal into 1 cm (^{1}/$_2$ inch) slices. Cut carrots as for parsnips. Set aside.
3 In medium-size skillet, melt 3 tablespoons butter over medium heat. When butter stops sizzling but before it browns, add parsnip and carrot slices, stirring to coat evenly with butter. Reduce heat to medium-low and cook, turning occasionally, about 5 minutes, or until vegetables are brown at the edges. Season with pepper to taste and sprinkle with 1 tablespoon parsley. Cover and set aside.
4 Preheat oven to SLOW.
5 Heat large skillet over medium-high heat. Add clarified butter and, just as it begins to smoke, add chicken breasts, smooth side down. Sauté chicken about 3 minutes, or until brown on one side. With tongs, turn chicken, tilt skillet to redistribute butter evenly in pan, and sauté on second side about 2 minutes. Turn chicken and continue to cook, turning, until meat in centre is still slightly pink and moist, another 2 to 5 minutes.
6 Divide chicken among individual dinner plates and keep warm in oven until ready to serve.
7 Reduce heat to medium, add 125 ml (4 fl oz) dry white wine, and deglaze pan. Increase heat to high and cook until wine is reduced by half, about 3 minutes. Add stock and reduce again by half.
8 Remove skillet from heat. One tablespoon at a time, stir in 175 g (6 oz) of prepared summer savory butter. When totally incorporated, pour just enough sauce over vegetables to coat them.
9 Remove dinner plates from oven and turn on grill.
10 Spoon remaining sauce over chicken breast halves. Spoon carrots and parsnips around chicken, sprinkle with remaining parsley, and serve.

Summer Savory Butter

1 lemon
1 tablespoon minced fresh summer savory, or 2 teaspoons dried
175 g (6 oz) unsalted butter
1 to 2 large shallots, peeled and minced
1 clove garlic, peeled and minced
2 level tablespoons chopped fresh parsley

1 Squeeze lemon and set juice aside. If using dried summer savory, combine with lemon juice in small bowl to allow herb flavour to develop.
2 Using food processor or electric mixer and bowl, cream butter until smooth.
3 Add shallots, garlic, parsley, and summer savory to butter and beat just until blended.
4 One teaspoon at a time, add lemon juice, or lemon juice with dried summer savory, and beat until blended. Turn into bowl, cover, and refrigerate.

Aligot

3 large boiling potatoes (about 625 g (1^1/$_4$ lbs) total weight)
Salt
3 level tablespoons unsalted butter
1 bunch scallions
125 g (^{1}/$_4$ lb) Cheddar cheese
125 g (^{1}/$_4$ lb) lean ham
1 clove garlic, peeled and minced
1 teaspoon ground coriander

1 Peel potatoes and cut into 4 cm (1^1/$_2$ inch) cubes. In medium-size saucepan, bring potatoes, 1 teaspoon salt, and water to cover to a boil over high heat. Lower heat to medium and boil, covered, 10 to 12 minutes, or until tender.
2 Meanwhile, melt butter in small heavy-gauge saucepan or butter warmer over low heat. Wash scallions and pat dry. Trim ends and cut scallions into 5 mm (^{1}/$_4$ inch) thick pieces to measure 125 g (4 oz). Grate cheese in processor or on coarse side of grater. Slice ham into 1 cm (^{1}/$_2$ inch) thick cubes.
3 Drain potatoes of all but 2 to 3 tablespoons of liquid and mash coarsely.
4 Add cheese, ham, garlic, coriander, and all but 2 tbsps scallions to potatoes, and stir until combined.
5 Turn potatoes into flameproof serving dish and sprinkle with melted butter and remaining scallions. Cover with foil and keep warm.
6 Just before serving, brown under grill for 2 minutes.

<table>
<tr><td>

</td><td>

Menu 3

Veal Scallops with Saffron Apples
Lentils with Tomatoes and Bacon
Sorrel and Celery Root Salad

</td></tr>
</table>

The sautéed veal scallops cook through quickly if you gently flatten them to a uniform thickness. Ask your butcher for veal scallops, cut from the loin, that are almost white. Make sure they are trimmed of any fat or silvery membrane. Before sautéeing the scallops, pat them dry so the butter does not spatter when you place them in the pan. To seal in the juices, avoid overcrowding the pieces.

The sauce for the veal contains *crème fraîche* and saffron, the world's costliest spice. *Crème fraîche* is a thickened cultured cream product with a slightly tart nutty taste. At one time available only in France, *crème fraîche* is now found in most supermarkets or speciality food shops. Both the green and the red lentils called for in the warm salad are imports, usually available at health food stores only. Regular supermarket lentils are acceptable, if not quite as flavourful and attractive.

Both the sorrel and celery root, or celeriac, in the salad are typically French vegetables. Sorrel, or sour grass, is a tart perennial herb that resembles spinach. If you substitute spinach, increase the amount of lemon juice and vinegar in the dressing to 1 tablespoon each. Celery root tastes a bit like nutty celery. Buy it no longer than 10 cm (4 inches) in diameter or the flesh will be woody. Since the skin is very thick, you will trim away almost half of the root when you peel it.

What to drink

A full-bodied white Burgundy would be a perfect accompaniment for this meal. A good-quality California Chardonnay would also be excellent.

Start-to-Finish Steps

The day before: If making your own crème fraîche, combine 250 ml (8 fl oz) heavy cream and 250 ml (8 fl oz) sour cream at room temperature in small bowl and whisk until blended. Turn into glass jar, cover tightly, and let stand at room temperature 6 to 8 hours. Refrigerate until ready to use.

One hour ahead: For lentils recipe, set out 22 level tablespoons butter to reach room temperature.

Fifteen minutes ahead: Clarify 6 level tablespoons butter for veal.

1   Follow salad recipe steps 1 to 5.

Saffron-tinted apple slices contrast handsomely with veal scallions for this Auvergnac-style meal. Serve the tossed sorrel and celery root salad and the lentils with tomatoes and bacon in separate wooden bowls.

2   Follow lentils recipe steps 1 to 4.

3   While tomato mixture is simmering, follow veal recipe steps 1 to 3.

4   Follow lentils recipe steps 5 to 7.

5   While lentils are simmering, follow salad recipe steps 6 to 8.

6   Follow lentils recipe step 8 and veal recipe steps 4 to 7.

7   Follow salad recipe step 9, veal recipe step 8, and serve with lentils.

Veal Scallops with Saffron Apples

Large lemon
4 medium-size tart apples, such as Granny Smith (about 1 kg (2 lbs) total weight)
1 to 2 large shallots
2 cloves garlic
1 teaspoon saffron threads
8 to 12 veal scallops (about 750 g (1½ lbs) total weight)
60 g (2 oz) flour for dredging
6 level tablespoons unsalted butter, clarified
100 ml (3 fl oz) dry white wine or dry white vermouth
125 ml (4 fl oz) veal or chicken stock, preferably homemade
250 ml (8 fl oz) crème fraîche or heavy cream

1   Preheat oven to SLOW.

2   Squeeze lemon, reserving 2 teaspoons juice for salad dressing. Wash, halve, and core apples; cut into 5 mm (¼ inch) thick wedges. Peel and mince enough shallots to measure 30 g (1 oz). Peel and mince garlic. Combine apples, lemon juice, shallots, garlic, and saffron in large mixing bowl and toss to combine; set aside.

3   Trim veal of any fat or membrane. With a wooden mallet or rolling pin, flatten, but do not pound, veal scallops to a uniform thickness of about 5 mm (¼ inch).

4   Place 60 g (2 oz) flour in pie pan and lightly dredge veal scallops on both sides. Shake off excess flour and set aside on large flat plate.

5   In large heavy-gauge skillet, heat 3 to 4 tablespoons clarified butter over medium-high heat. Place as many scallops in skillet as will fit without overcrowding, increase heat to high, and brown veal quickly, 2 to 3 minutes on each side, adding more clarified butter as needed. With tongs, transfer scallops to heatproof serving platter and keep warm in oven. Repeat for remaining scallops.

6   For sauce, carefully pour off any fat and butter remaining in skillet. Add wine and deglaze pan over medium-high heat, scraping up any browned bits clinging to bottom of pan with a wooden spatula. Cook until liquid is reduced to 2 tablespoons, about 2 minutes. Add veal or chicken stock. From serving platter, pour accumulated veal juices back into skillet. Increase heat to high and cook, stirring, until sauce is reduced to 60 ml (2 fl oz), about 2 minutes.

7   Add crème fraîche, or heavy cream, to reduced stock, and cook at just under boiling point until sauce thickens, 3 to 5 minutes.

8   Add apple mixture to sauce and stir gently until combined. Reduce heat and simmer gently until apples are heated through, about 2 minutes. Pour sauce over veal scallops, top with apples, and serve immediately.

Lentils with Tomatoes and Bacon

355 g (¾ lb) green or red lentils
Salt
250 g (½ lb) smoked slab bacon, unsliced
Small onion
2 large tomatoes
½ teaspoon dried sage
½ teaspoon dried rosemary
60 ml (2 fl oz) dry white vermouth
Small bunch parsley
2 level tablespoons unsalted butter

1   Pick over lentils to remove pebbles or other foreign matter. Place lentils in large sieve and rinse thoroughly under cold running water. Transfer to medium-size heavy-gauge saucepan. Add ½ teaspoon salt and water to cover, and bring to a boil over high heat, skimming off any scum that rises to surface.

2   While lentils are coming to a boil, slice bacon into 1 cm (½ inch) cubes, about 1¼ cups. Peel and chop enough onion to measure 45 g (1½ oz). Wash tomatoes and pat dry. Peel, core, halve, seed, and chop tomatoes; set aside.

3   Boil lentils 1 minute, cover, and remove from heat.

4   In medium-size heavy-gauge skillet, fry bacon cubes over medium heat until crisp, about 5 minutes. Add onion and sauté until onion is translucent, about 3 minutes. Carefully pour off bacon fat from skillet. Add tomatoes, sage, rosemary, and vermouth, and simmer until nearly all liquid has evaporated, about 15 minutes. Set aside.

5   In large sieve, drain lentils and rinse under cold

running water. Return lentils to saucepan, add fresh water to cover by 2¹/₂ cm (1 inch), and bring lentils to a boil over high heat.

6 While lentils are coming to a boil, wash parsley and pat dry with paper towels. Chop enough parsley to measure 2 tablespoons.

7 Lower heat under lentils to a simmer, cover, and cook gently until tender, about 10 minutes for green lentils or 4 minutes for red lentils.

8 Transfer lentils to sieve, drain thoroughly, and turn into heatproof serving bowl. Add bacon-tomato mixture, butter, and chopped parsley, and toss gently to combine. Keep warm in SLOW oven until ready to serve.

Sorrel and Celery Root Salad

60 ml (2 fl oz) plus 2 tablespoons olive oil
2 teaspoons tarragon vinegar
2 teaspoons lemon juice
2 teaspoons Dijon mustard
1 teaspoon dry mustard
1 level tablespoon anchovy paste
1 cucumber
Large red bell pepper
1 celery root (about 750 g (1¹/₂ lbs))
350 g (³/₄ lb) fresh sorrel or spinach
1 clove garlic
60 g (2 oz) Parmesan cheese
Salt and freshly ground black pepper

1 For dressing, combine olive oil, vinegar, lemon juice, mustards, and anchovy paste in small jar with tight-fitting lid, and shake until thoroughly blended. Set aside at room temperature.

2 Peel cucumber, halve lengthwise, and scrape out seeds with teaspoon or melon baller. Cut halves into 1 cm (¹/₂ inch) thick crescents. Place in colander, sprinkle with 1 tablespoon salt, and set aside to drain.

3 Wash red pepper and pat dry. Core, seed, and cut pepper into 2¹/₂ cm (1 inch) squares. Place pepper in small bowl, drizzle with 2 to 3 tablespoons dressing, toss gently, and set aside.

4 In small saucepan, bring 1¹/₄ ltrs (2 pts) of water to a boil over high heat. While water is heating, peel celery root and cut in half. Cut halves into 5 mm (¹/₄ inch) thick slices, then into julienne strips. Plunge celery root into boiling water and blanch 10 seconds. Transfer to sieve and refresh under cold running water. Drain thoroughly, wrap in paper towels, and refrigerate until ready to assemble salad.

5 Wash sorrel, or spinach, if using, and remove any

discoloured leaves. Dry in salad spinner or pat dry with paper towels. Wrap in paper towels and refrigerate.

6 Peel garlic clove and rub over inside surface of wooden salad bowl. Discard garlic. Cover bowl and set aside.

7 In food processor or with grater, grate enough Parmesan to measure 2 tablespoons.

8 Rinse cucumber under cold running water to remove salt. Place in cloth napkin or kitchen towel and squeeze out any excess moisture. Add cucumbers to peppers and toss.

9 Place sorrel and celery root in salad bowl. Shake dressing to recombine, pour over sorrel and celery root, and toss. Top with peppers and cucumbers, sprinkle with Parmesan, and season with black pepper to taste.

Added touch
When washing beaters, be sure to remove any trace of yolk before beating the whites or you will not achieve the volume necessary for this chilled soufflé.

Iced Lemon Soufflé

2 medium-size lemons
125 ml (4 fl oz) heavy cream
1 teaspoon vanilla extract
5 eggs
125 g (4 oz) sugar
Pinch of salt
1 envelope unflavoured gelatine

1 Juice 1 lemon and set aside. Grate enough of remaining lemon to measure 1 level tablespoon zest.

2 Lightly grease inside of medium-size soufflé dish with vegetable oil or butter. Tie a waxed-paper collar around top of soufflé dish.

3 In bowl of electric mixer, whip heavy cream with vanilla until stiff. Turn into medium-size bowl.

4 Separate eggs, sliding yolks into a small bowl and whites into a large bowl. Add sugar to yolks and beat at high speed 10 minutes, or until mixture becomes very thick.

5 Wash beaters thoroughly and whip egg whites with salt until they form stiff peaks.

6 Using rubber spatula, gently fold whipped cream into egg whites. Add thickened egg yolk mixture and lemon zest, and fold just until incorporated.

7 In small pan, combine lemon juice with gelatine. Warm slightly over low heat until gelatine dissolves. When cool, gently stir gelatine into soufflé mixture.

8 Turn mixture into soufflé dish and refrigerate at least 2 hours before serving.

Meet the Cooks

Carol Brendlinger and Michael Wild

What started as a hobby for Carol Brendlinger, who grew up in Pennsylvania, and Michael Wild, who was born in France, has become a profession and a way of life for them both. They are both chefs, and Carol Brendlinger also teaches cookery classes and develops recipes for numerous publications.

Jeanne Voltz

Jeanne Voltz has been the food editor of *The Miami Herald* and *The Los Angeles Times*. She is also the author of various cookery books and a founding member of the New York City chapter of Les Dames d'Escoffier.

Leslee Reis

Leslee Reis is the owner and head chef of Café Provençal in Illinois. She has worked as a caterer, a restaurant consultant, and a teacher of French cooking, and has been cited by the media numerous times for her contributions to the food profession.

Jacques Mokrani

Jacques Mokrani, who was born in Algiers, attended the hotel and restaurant school of the Société Hôtelière in Marseilles, France. Later he served as an apprentice at the Savoy Grill in London. In 1973, he opened his own restaurant, LaBoucane, in San Francisco.

John Case

Born in Maine, John Case first worked as a part-time apprentice and restaurant manager, before becoming head chef at the Mountainside Inn in Point Pleasant, Pennsylvania. He is currently chef and club manager at a country club in Pennsylvania.

Dennis Gilbert

After graduating, Dennis Gilbert decided to combine two careers: cooking and writing. He apprenticed with a chef in Maine and trained in restaurants specializing in classical and regional French cooking. He is now *chef de cuisine* at the Vinyard Restaurant in Maine, and teaches English at the University of Southern Maine.

A Wealth of Herbs

Increasingly, herbs are arriving in the markets fresh; the proliferation of health stores and other specialist shops has widened choice, and many cooks with gardens have taken to raising their own. Recent ethnic influences have called attention to once seemingly esoteric herbs. Coriander, for one, is at last gaining deserved popularity in Europe, although cooks in Asia and the Middle East have been using it for centuries.

Anyone wishing to dry fresh herbs can tie them loosely in a bundle and hang them upside down in a cool, dark, well-ventilated place for several weeks. When the leaves are completely dried, strip them from the stems and store them in an airtight container.

Two swifter methods of preserving herbs make use of the microwave oven and the freezer. To microwave herbs, place five or six sprigs at a time between paper towels and microwave them on high for 1 to 3 minutes until the leaves are brittle. Store the leaves loosely in airtight jars.

To freeze herbs, rinse the sprigs and pat them dry. Strip the leaves off the stems and put them into a heavy-duty plastic bag. Gently flatten the bag to force out the air, seal the bag tightly, and place it in your freezer. Use the leaves as the need arises.

Basil (also called sweet basil): This fragrant herb, with its underlying flavour of anise and hint of clove, goes particularly well with tomato.

Chervil: The small, lacy leaves of this herb have a taste akin to parsley with a touch of anise. It is good in salads and salad dressings. Chervil is popular in France where it is often an ingredient in herb mixtures, including *fines herbes*. When used in cooking, chervil should be added at the end, lest its subtle flavour be lost.

Chives: The smallest of the onions, chives grow in grassy clumps. When finely cut, the hollow leaves contribute their delicate, oniony flavour to fresh salads and raw vegetables. Chives should always be used fresh, as dried ones are virtually tasteless.

Coriander (also called cilantro): The serrated leaves of the coriander plant impart a distinctive fragrance and a flavour that is both mildly sweet and bitter. Coriander leaves should be used fresh or added at the end of cooking if their flavour is to be appreciated fully.

Dill: A sprightly herb with feathery leaves, dill enhances cucumber and many other fresh vegetables, as well as fish and shellfish. When used in cooking, dill should be added towards the end of the process to preserve its delicate flavour. Both dill seeds and dill leaves can be